QUINTESSENTIALLY

Weddings

LONDON

29 Portland Place
London W1B 1QB
United Kingdom
+44 845 475 8400
london@quintessentiallyweddings.com

GENEVA

Rue de Lausanne 69
1202 Geneva
Switzerland
+41 840 316 316
geneva@quintessentiallyweddings.com

NEW DELHI

115, 2nd Floor, Institutional Area
Sector - 44, Gurgaon - 122002
New Delhi
India
+91 124 485 6605
newdelhi@quintessentiallyweddings.com

HONG KONG

2/F Teda Building
87 Wing Lok Street, Sheung Wan
Hong Kong
+852 3758 7422
hongkong@quintessentiallyweddings.com

SINGAPORE

1 North Bridge Road
6-31 High Street Centre
179094
Singapore
+65 9068 1624
singapore@quintessentiallyweddings.com

THE SECRET
QUINTESSENTIALLY
Weddings
GUIDE

Contents

THE WEDDING CONCEPTS

About the Author

Sophie McCorry Day is part of the Quintessentially Weddings team. A Fine Art graduate of Chelsea College of Art, she could not dispel a love of writing; she went on to achieve a qualification in Journalism from London College of Communication. She has experience at many of the major fashion titles, from Vogue to the Guardian's Fashion and Feature desks, Harper's Bazaar and Grazia. In addition, she still practises creatively and has worked in PR, Events and copywriting for luxury brands. At the time of going to press she had just become Sophie McCorry Day, having written this book whilst simultaneously planning her own wedding; a fact which placed her in a unique position our resident bride blogger and as a creative stylist for weddings.

Foreword

Congratulations! If you are just engaged, are re-marrying or are simply a keen parent or friend of the bride or groom, welcome to the ride of your life. More than ever before, weddings capture our hearts and imaginations. Whether you aspire to the lavish but lovely wedding of the Duke and Duchess of Cambridge; a countryside affair with a vogueish twist or even a destination wedding on a far flung beach, every wedding contains a dose of magic.

However, nothing quite prepares you for the trials and tribulation of planning a wedding. The pitfalls and pressures are everywhere for the more impressionable among us: think of all of the wedding blogs out there, not to mention the ubiquitous celebrity wedding. Along with the obligatory elements of planning, it is little wonder that even those with nerves of steel can be left flustered by the entire process. That is where this book, The Secret Quintessentially Weddings Guide, comes in.

Over the coming pages we are going to show you more than 200 stylish and extraordinary ideas, insider secrets, scheduling tips, shopping suggestions and beautiful images to inspire you and make planning your wedding a breeze.

Including a selection of our hand-picked, favourite suppliers, designers and beautiful venues, you will find all of the legendary, luxury industry greats in here. There are also names and gems of ideas you will never have heard of. Let the wedding planning begin!

Sophie McCorry Day

Introduction

What makes a perfect wedding?

Whether you have dreamt of your big day since you were little or are new to the world of weddings and what we call 'wedmin', your wedding will be a once-in-a-lifetime experience of joy, beauty and romance; unique, because it's yours. Here, at Quintessentially Weddings we have years of experience designing, planning and producing religious weddings, civil ceremonies and partnerships, blessings, celebration parties and receptions across the world for all denominations. We like to think our wedding are as fabulous as love and marriage itself. Put simply, we love weddings.

Quintessentially Weddings was founded in 2006 by Anabel Fielding and Caroline Hurley as a global sister company to Quintessentially Events. The mission was to move away from the usual traditions with an emphasis on luxurious style

and a personal, bespoke approach. We create sumptuous weddings that not only stand the test of time (you'll hopefully look back on your wedding photographs in 50 years' time and still catch your breath with how beautiful it all was) but have that touch of the extraordinary.

We match-make every supplier, each little detail, monogram and arrangement to suit you and your wedding guests' needs. Be it the classical beauty of grand venues such as Wrotham Park or contemporary and fashion-forward venues like Babington House, we can find the perfect setting anywhere in the world. For your dress we have our own resident fashion stylist Katy Scarlet Taylor to guide you around some of our favourite boutiques such as Browns Bride, Vivienne Westwood and Matthew Williamson.

We are lucky to work with some of the world's foremost wedding suppliers, venues, entertainers, wedding fashion designers and talent when planning weddings all over the world.

Our strong relationships with these partners afford us amazing preferential rates and everyone goes the extra mile to pull together the most incredible weddings for the love of it. We embrace nothing more than taking a 'blank canvas' space that has perhaps never hosted a wedding before, and bringing it to life. We have a dedicated, passionate team of planners who support, guide and plot every day to turn dreams into a reality. Our team can even jump on board at the last minute should your energy start to flag, and be as involved and close as you wish, or simply support when you need it most. That is what we do, and we adore it.

SOME OF OUR WEDDING WONDERS

Mr & Mrs Mansour

"Your attention to detail throughout the entire project and positive attitude helped to make the lead-up to the wedding day a pleasure and a joy. Your hard work and exceptional efforts throughout the past few months have been amazing."

Lauren Gurvich & Jeremy King

"We want to thank you from the bottom of our hearts for all of the very hard work you put into this event. Everyone was so impressed by everything and it was the best day of our lives. Magical place, wonderful people, splendid weather, spectacular food and perfect production!"

Yasmin & Mads Jensen

"I wanted to send you the very biggest of thanks for helping us organise such a superb and exceptional wedding. We have been showered with superlatives and this is in large part due to the extraordinary efforts of you and the team. Thank you!"

Mary-Clare & Ben Elliot

"We will be forever grateful for all the support, wisdom and creativity the Quintessentially Weddings team showed us all on the best day of our lives."

Evgenia & Pierre

"We couldn't even dream about such a magical wedding. Thank you for making it happen, it was amazing, beyond our wildest dreams. I think we'll remember every second of it for the rest of our lives, and I have the feeling that our guests will too."

Linda & Tony Bloom

"I am totally overwhelmed and speechless about the awesomeness of what you are creating for us. Thank you and the team so much for all your hard work. You are truly geniuses."

WHY THIS BOOK?

For those who are not natural born organisers, planning your wedding can seem an incredible feat. There is everything to think of from the wording of the invitations to guest list politics; the role of a good groom to choosing a dress. Then you have to prioritise, plot, negotiate, barter, hunt, revise, pay, source, pursue, placate, order, style, take deliveries, dress, collect, assimilate, complete the legal paperwork, negotiate some more, and bring it all together on time and in budget. No wonder it seems exhausting just to look at and that so many brides and grooms are accused of being 'Bridezillas' or 'Groomlins' when it all gets too much.

That's why we came up with The Secret Quintessentially Weddings Guide. This book is purely designed to help you, because life's too short to worry about what should be one of the happiest and most special days of your life. We want to guide you through choosing your engagement ring (if you haven't already) right up to planning your trousseau and honeymoon.

We wish you the very best of luck, and of course you can always call on us if you need to.

Anabel Fielding   *Caroline Hurley*

Introduction to Part One

It begins: from the engagement
rocks that will make you weak at the knees to the
etiquette, ins and outs of invitations, hunting out that
perfect venue to those teeny tiny finishing touches
that polish off your big day in style. Here follows a
step-by-step guide to creating your perfect wedding.
With the help of industry stars, some known,
some not so, this first half is designed to help you
go beyond the essentials to the real nitty-gritty of
successful haggling and insider tips to help fulfil all
of your big day dreams. Kicking off with all things
that sparkle in our Engagement Rocks guide to rings
and, of course, the jewels to seal the deal we will
take you right through to those final few moments
before you say 'I do' and even afterwards with tips
to a happy marriage and anniversary gift ideas to
keep that smile on your face for years to come. As
someone wise once said, no pain, no gain – and
whilst we cannot promise your wedding planning
will be bereft of trickier moments, we hope that the
following chapters will make it as easy as can be.

Engagement
Rocks

De Beers

What makes the perfect

engagement ring? Take the 'four C's' of cut, clarity, carat and colour, add a delicate setting and no small amount of flawless brilliance and you may come close. For the ultimate symbol of true love, a De Beers jewel possesses a certain timeless magic, with a twist of contemporary appeal. Known as The Jeweller of Light, De Beers perpetuates a 120-year old heritage of diamond mastery that shines through with each of its rings. The in-house craftsmen fuse these tried-and-tested traditions with modern high-tech precision, resulting in an unprecedented level of refinement. Starting with the diamonds (which have to pass the in-house test of Fire, Life and Brilliance before being stamped with an imperceptible DB marque) your chosen engagement band can be as individual as you, although as the President of the De Beers Institute of Diamonds puts it: "Ultimately, it is the diamond that chooses you!".

From iconic DB Classic rings with a brilliant solitaire bursting from assorted platinum bands, to The Promise collection with bands featuring a modern asymmetric twist of interlocking arms, and the sumptuous Aura range of cushion-cut diamonds or even coloured engagement rings set with radiant yellow and pink diamonds. A De Beers engagement ring is our go-to for elegance, purity and natural beauty. Each band is created from platinum, the rarest of precious metals for durability and faultless style that makes every ring a classic to cherish for the rest of your life (with not a scratch to show for it). Diamonds are forever, after all…

For the wedding day itself, there are glimmering wedding 'court' bands in platinum, white gold and coloured gold for both brides and grooms to seal the deal. Or you could make a statement by pairing your engagement ring with a band of coloured pavé round-cut diamonds for real 'wow' factor – try both understated traditional bands and embellished versions on when choosing your engagement ring to get the full vision of how they will look together. How to set off your wedding dress perfectly? Complete your look with an Enchanted Lotus necklace with diamond droplets tracing down to a lotus flower, perhaps a twinkling wreath bracelet of diamond blossom, or just add a dollop of glamour with some simple sleeper studs from the complete bridal line.

How to Choose your De Beers Engagement Ring

Using unique Iris technology, now you can see the perfection of your diamonds through the eyes of the jewellers who look for the signature Fire, Life and Brilliance. For non-experts, Fire describes the way diamonds refract light for the kaleidoscope of colours you see bouncing around a room when light hits the diamonds, Life the sparkle and Brilliance the diamonds' natural beauty.

Don't expect to choose the ring you had in mind – always try on the wildcard and different settings as you never know what might catch your eye.

Discuss your budget and go with a clear limit in mind if you're choosing together. Make a day of it, and give yourself a lunch-break with time to go away and think about your choice.

Try on the more spectacular rings – this is a 'forever' piece you're choosing, so plump for something that you'll never want to take off. And it's all about that smile – if you can't stop smiling when you think about your ring, it's the one!

Boucheron

How to ensure your ring wows for a lifetime? By choosing a Boucheron brilliant, of course.

This is the jeweller who once brought one of France's crown jewels (and a very large, high carat diamond at that) and not as some assumed, at the request of a super-wealthy private bidder; but to set it into a ring for his own beloved wife. Small wonder then that the house of Boucheron has been known ever since as the jeweller of love and a go-to for the man truly head-over-heels.

Established over 150 years ago in Paris, this world renowned Maison is still steeped in the selfsame spirit of romance and refined beauty that marked out its namesake Frederic Boucheron's jewellery. From fantastical high jewellery that features vibrantly coloured jewel-dusted flamingos and swans to twinkling engagement rings as individual yet eternally stylish as they come, these are forever pieces expertly crafted with real affection.

Needless to say you can almost feel the care in selecting only the most star-like of stones, and setting them in exquisite bands which often feature novel textural detail or tiny diamonds visible only from the underside of the ring's arms.

The Ava collection of round and teardrop stones set in halos of pavé diamonds and statement 'Quatre Folies' solitaires are wonderfully sparkling on their own, but when paired with matching wedding bands with which to pledge your troth, are almost as blinding as love itself.

Leviev

For bridal jewellery as luxurious, glittering and extraordinary as it comes, look no further than the precious pieces from Leviev. Bridging the gap between high-end jewellery hand-crafted with traditional skills and some of the rarest stones in the world (with supersized, fancy and coloured diamonds a speciality) and a fashion sensibility, these are rings and gems in which to play out your every Elizabeth Taylor fantasy. But whilst the design aesthetic of Leviev is admittedly glamorous, the proportion, balance and exquisite settings in Platinum or 18 carat gold exemplify classic upscale jewellery, with just a bit of a flamboyant edge to make each piece feel truly one-off.

There are more traditional engagement rings of large cushion cut or square emerald-cut diamonds framed by lustrous bands of pavé brilliants or tapered baguette stones. However, if idiosyncratic jewels that reflect your personality are more your thing, look to the fancy yellow, pear or marquise cut stones that are each and every one classified by gemologists as 'flawless' – the pinnacle of diamond purity. We discovered Leviev as their London boutique opened in 2006 and have loved them ever since; in particular for their flower rings of blue and petal-shaped white diamonds and the cluster rings of round-cut brilliants topped with a dazzling central stone.

If you are searching for something as unique as you are, these make discerning choices for an unusual engagement ring.

The full collection of drop necklaces, chandelier earrings, pendants set on chains or gems forming lustrous bracelets fit the bill for accessorising your big-day outfit, and there are even discreet gem-studded cufflinks for grooms. The Haute Joaillerie range boasts decadent jewels in vivid yellow, pink and emerald in addition to a 20 carat flawless diamond ring that is by far and away the most knockout we've seen, but executed in such fine style so as not to be showy. Every Leviev diamond is conflict-free and ethically sourced, with unique stones sourced in a considered fashion that means the only qualm you should have when choosing your ring is whether to live out your crown-jewel dreams or opt for a slightly more understated, but no less fabulous ring to rock.

29 Portland Place

Welcome to our selection of some of the best venues for your engagement party, starting with our very own 29 Portland Place.

All things bright and beautiful - 29 Portland Place encapsulates Georgian elegance. An imposing town house in the heart of London, it is one of the few surviving Robert Adam private residences with plenty of delicious period detail. A recent restoration has reawakened its original grandeur, with polished front doors opening to reveal a black and white chequered marble floor, a sweeping staircase and two sets of high-ceilinged and sunny ballrooms in aurora borealis shades of eau de nil, Wedgwood blue, peppermint and starch-white courtesy of Farrow & Ball. Add to this twinkling chandeliers and stucco flourishes and these ballrooms couldn't be more perfect for an engagement soiree.

What with all the elaborate details of the interiors here, flowers and finishing touches needn't cost a fortune either, as the venue does all of the work for you. 29 Portland Place partners with a select handful of caterers, florists, bar and lighting teams guaranteeing the most all-round elegant party for those in the know. It is available either as a dry hire space, or replete with its in-house event manager, with a capacity of 110 guests standing across the two ballrooms; the larger space housed on the first floor holds 100 standing, or 80 seated. Why not host a cocktail and canapé reception in the ground floor ballrooms before ascending to dinner and dancing (lots of dancing) in the upper ballroom?

Insider Tip

"Did you know that in the past, the bride's parents would host a party to secretly announce the engagement, and guests would not know the cause of the celebrations to which they were invited? Reawaken the traditional surprise and keep your guests in the dark about the party's motive – there will be tears!"

Hawksmoor

Let's be honest – weddings themselves aren't the most masculine of things. But truly breath taking food (and meat especially) will disarm even the least romantic of men – and if ever there was a way to a man's heart, Hawksmoor is it.

The collection of fine steakhouses that stud the heart of London make for perfect engagement party, rehearsal dinner and even wedding reception venues with its Guildhall restaurant boasting a private dining room replete with its own bar for 22 guests for an intimate celebration. With their New York grit meets gloss interiors – all mirrors and walnut panelling that look particularly stylish when softly lit and adorned with cut-crystal vases of flowers to bring a little prettiness to proceedings, you can take over Hawksmoor Guildhall on weekends for anything up to 300 people for a drink and canapé party. The newly opened Spitalfields basement bar is perhaps the most glamorous, with its golden pineapples (a traditional part of any wedding, as a symbol of welcome) and copper-topped tables set against inky midnight walls and libations of marmalade cocktails, juleps and Champagne muddled with fruits and spirits. The food itself is simply sublime; and though the steak is prized as the best in London, there is plenty of lighter, female-friendly fare (or you could just opt to indulge).

From the legendary triple-cooked chips (a trick borrowed from their friend Heston Blumenthal) or even lobster grilled with hazelnut butter, to Chateaubriand, Porterhouse, D-Rump, Fillet and T-Bone steaks so dark, handsome, velvety and flavoursome, the food here will sweep you off your Jimmy Choos. Then there are those delectable puddings of Drunken Sticky Toffee pudding with a positively naughty sauce, Peanut Butter and Salted Caramel Shortbread served with Salted Caramel Ice-Cream. This is comfort food, but not as you or your guests know it, for it's the luxurious version. Paired with beautiful Rieslings and Malbecs matched to your menu, the foodie's wedding has never looked nor tasted so good.

D&D London

When it comes to celebrating
your engagement, hosting a stag, hen night or a
rehearsal wedding dinner, D & D London hold
an impressive portfolio of refined and glamorous
restaurants. Be it a grand dinner in a classic French
restaurant or a relaxed gathering overlooking the
Thames, there's a D & D spot for you.

There are 33 private and semi-private dining
spaces available across London, all of which can
be dressed to fit your wedding aesthetic with
flowers, drapery and entertainment curated by
the in-house teams. If you want to give guests a
taste of what's in store on your wedding day, the
venues and feel can also be styled accordingly.

Every D & D London venue caters for fully
personalised menus. From the modern refinement
of Launceston Place, the buzz of the Chelsea
hotspot Bluebird, the iconic Quaglino's in St
James and the contemporary French ambiance
at Coq d'Argent - each restaurant is distinctive
and unique. The collection reads a little like
a gastronomic tour of Europe (with the exotic
addition of India at Carom). Who wouldn't
accept an invitation to dine on a menu that reads
something like this? Risotto with wild mushrooms,
aged parmesan and truffle cream at Sauterelle,
oysters or Belgian endive and papillon Roquefort
with candied walnuts washed down with lashings
of Champagne at Quaglino's, or red wine-
poached foie gras with pear and Riesling jelly at
Orrery. Then there are the puddings we'd fight
tooth and nail for: Michelin-starred Launceston
Place's Valrhona chocolate soufflé with praline
ganache, only mildly eclipsed by the mini éclairs
and raspberry shortcake canapés at Bluebird. You
can even hold your marriage ceremony at the
Bluebird in Chelsea, Avenue in Mayfair or Plateau
with its glossy Canary Wharf setting as all three
are licensed for civil ceremonies.

Planning &
Ceremonies

Wedding Diary

The dresses, the bouquets, the stately homes. Where to start? Right here for our insider's guide to planning your wedding:

12 Months and Under
- Dream: pool all of your ideas and inspiration together.
- Throw an engagement soiree.
- Work out your maximum budget; put what you can in an easy-access ISA to earn interest (and extra spend).
- Choose a wedding planner if you wish to use one.
- Draw up your guestlist.
- Visit ceremony and reception venues from your shortlist, and make provisional bookings.
- Set the date and time with your vicar, rabbi, registrar or celebrant.
- Book photographers and videographers: the most talented are snapped up many months ahead.
- Start thinking about your dress: a note of caution, many bridal shops are booked up months in advance and Saturday appointments are like gold-dust. Visit during the quieter week days if you can.

11-10 Months
- Send out Save the Dates.
- Book flights and connections for the wedding party for destination weddings to ensure you are all there on time and within budget (the cost of flights to some destinations will soar closer to the time).
- Finalise your wedding party: the bridesmaids,

flower girls, groomsmen, best man and maid of honour.
- Start any fitness or beauty regimes now for optimum results.
- Choose your dress if you can, allowing at least six months for made-to-measure and the full ten months for special commissions (but don't worry, some boutiques can turn dresses around in three months at a push).

10-8 Months
- Find your florist and discuss your bouquets, buttonholes and the arrangements for the venues.
- Choose and order your wedding cake.
- Go bridesmaid dress shopping.
- Visit your caterer for a tasting and select your final menu.
- Grooms should order bespoke suits.
- If you have a 'dry-hire' venue, hire lighting, PA systems, a dance floor, furniture, crockery and linen.
- Start choosing readings, hymns and music for your ceremony.

8-6 Months
- Choose your gift registry and shop for your gifts.
- Order your stationery.
- Book the wedding cars for the bride, parents and bridesmaids – and also any coaches or taxis required to ferry guests to the reception venue.
- Research local hotels and reserve rooms for your

wedding guests.
- Grooms and the groomsmen should order any hire suits or go shopping for off-the-peg outfits.
- Shop for your lingerie to go under the dress: you will need it for the first fitting.
- Meet your vicar, rabbi or celebrant and confirm your order of service, all music and timings.
- Go for your first facial, make-up trial and hair consultation.

6-4 Months
- Shop for your trousseau.
- Book your make-up artist.
- Grooms should choose and book the hotel for the wedding night.
- Issue invitations, with full venue details, local accommodation, gift registry and RSVP cards. Set an RSVP deadline one month from now.
- Confirm timings for the photography, and pass this information to your caterer and venue.
- Send off your passport for renewal in your new married name.
- Book any jabs you may need for exotic honeymoons and request visas too.

4-2 Months
- Organise a rehearsal dinner if you are hosting one.
- Colour your hair now to allow for time to get used to any change, and top-up closer to the big day.
- Dress up! Try your wedding dress on, move around and check you haven't forgotten anything.
- Order flower girl and page boy outfits to ensure they fit (any sooner and they may outgrow them).
- Chase any RSVP stragglers; draw up a final list of acceptances and refusals. Give to your caterer along with any details of food intolerances or specific diets.
- Go for your first dress fitting and specify alterations for a perfect fit.
- Order any games or entertainers to keep guests amused.
- Book hen and stag nights!

The Final Months
- Create your day's running order of timings such as your arrival at the ceremony, formal photography, food serving times, cake-cutting etc. and include a hot-list of your supplier's numbers.

- Begin writing any vows and speeches.
- Write names on place cards, and order your seating chart and table plaques.
- Give notice to marry if you are marrying anywhere other than a Church of England church at least 15 days before the wedding.
- Collect your wedding dress after any final alterations.
- Have a final cut and colour two weeks to ten days before the wedding; grooms should do likewise.
- Take any last trips to facialists, spas and choose your big day fragrance.
- Practice walking about the house with a sheet tied around your waist if you are having a train.
- Collect your cake, flowers, groomsmen's outfits and any last minute items one day before the wedding.

The Night Before
You'll feel altogether calmer, less jittery and more fabulous if you tuck yourself into bed for a good night's sleep at an early hour. Ditch the wine at the rehearsal dinner to avoid hangovers or pasty faces and banish the bloat by cutting out caffeine and processed sugar by lunchtime the day before. Grooms should (traditionally) sleep apart from the bride and have their best men with them to placate any nerves!

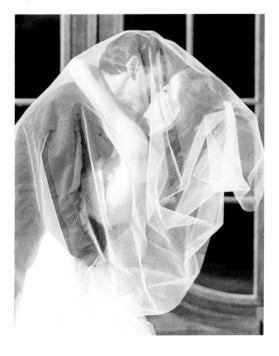

Ten Steps to Perfect Planning

Keep calm and marry on with our essential tips to planning your wedding and nailing wedmin…

1. Put all of your receipts, hot contacts, payment dates and essentials in a wedding planner – we love Smythson's beautiful Panama versions.

2. Always tackle the formal 'musts' of a wedding first, such as booking the ceremony, registrar and finding a caterer so guests are well-fed and watered before you plan the prettier bits.

3. The list is your friend. Divide tasks into short and long lead so you can see the wood for the trees.

4. Don't be afraid to delegate; but only the things you don't care too dearly about as someone else's taste and choice of flowers, music, cake or cocktails might niggle on the day.

5. Play safe, and have a contingency fund – 77% of weddings go over budget.

6. Hone your focus down to the three key things that you care most about for your wedding. If you cinch these, any extras are just added bonuses. If for instance you dream of a party ending in a flurry of fireworks, armfuls of Lily of the Valley or a Vera Wang frock, organise these first and foremost - keep your eyes on the prize.

7. When you are tempted to buy items or be seduced into overspending, stop and think 'Do I really love it? Can I imagine my wedding without it?' – if the answer is no, then by all means splurge but be prepared to make savings elsewhere to compensate.

8. Don't get caught up in fads or fashions: even Kate Moss kept her wedding timelessly elegant.

9. When making enquiries or haggling, don't mention the 'W' word but simply ask how much it would cost to hire, buy or rent for a 'private party' to gauge prices without the wedding mark-up. Once suppliers come back to you with a price, be nice but firm and offer 2/3 below your ceiling to open discussion. Try saying 'I was hoping for something more like £X….' and leave suppliers to decide whether to cut a deal.

10. Get good at asking. You'll be surprised at the extras some suppliers will offer if you ask nicely, and equally how bad some of them can be with providing receipts, confirmation of bookings etc. You're not being a nag or a bridezilla if you ask politely, just being sensible.

The Big Day

Welcome to the most beautiful, meaningful and truly romantic day of your life. Here's how to ensure it goes off immaculately…

9.00am When you wake, have a breakfast of something simple such as porridge with honey (a natural anti-inflammatory, it has a soothing effect on nervous tummies). Brides should have hair and make-up done last to extend its life, then dress.

12.30pm The groom, best men and ushers should be at the ceremony venue half an hour before it begins to welcome and seat guests. If you are using a wedding planner, they will be there to oversee the final touches.

1.10pm Traditionally the bride arrives 20 minutes late, but many venues, registrars (and grooms) will become worried; aim for ten minutes as a happy medium. When walking down the aisle, flower girls usually go first, followed by bridesmaids then the bride and the person giving her away, with the maid of honour last; but feel free to shake it up.

1.15pm The ceremony is at the heart of the day: dependent upon your order of service, it may take anything from 20 minutes to an hour and a half.

2.15pm If you are having formal photography, allocate up to half an hour for this, but provide refreshments for flagging relatives and friends.

2.45pm The reception: either host a traditional 'receiving line' to greet your guests, or keep it light with a Champagne and canapé reception.

4.00pm Breakfast is usually served an hour after guests have arrived. As the last course is cleared, the speeches commence with the bride's father followed by the bridegroom (who pays homage to his lovely new wife, her parents for their help and toasts the wedding party). Then finally, the naughtier speech from the best man who introduces the groom to the bride's family and tells witty anecdotes about the groom to illustrate how his new wife has redeemed him (jokes should be family-friendly).

7.00pm Cut your cake and serve with tea and coffee before the first dance as the lights are turned down low. Then the revelry begins! You could also opt for fireworks, cocktails, a photo booth session, and change into a frivolous dancing number should you have one.

Midnight After all the partying, it's a nice idea to pre-order taxis to whisk weary guests away. The bride and groom usually depart before the end of the party, traditionally with the bride tossing the bouquet as she leaves to a lucky girl (you can always ask for it back should you wish to preserve it). The wedding car should be adorned with 'Just Married' signs and rattling cans on string…

Ceremonies
I do, I do, I do

At the heart of your wedding day sits the ceremony; the part where the two of you declare your adoration of each other with pledges to love each other till the end in front of all your gathered loved ones. A wedding, after all, should open the doors to a marriage built on true love, friendship, partnership and constancy: whilst it's all too easy to get carried away by the giddy loveliness of planning the celebrations, if you choose a ceremony that fits your beliefs and hopes and is meaningful to you, you can't go far wrong.

These are the most popular ways to wed, and all the contacts you need to do it your way.

Civil Ceremony

For an informal and personalised ceremony with your own vows and readings added to the statutory declarations that make the marriage legal, this ceremony can be hosted in any venue that has acquired a licence under the UK Marriage Act. The only criteria is that your civil ceremony venue is a permanent building and free from any religious links: this means you can take your pick from romantic stately homes, garden follies (so you can marry in a garden, but under the auspices of a structure such as a summerhouse), registry offices, restaurants, moored boats, castles, quirky barns and luxury hotels. You will need to book an approved registrar to marry you, calling the council local to your chosen ceremony venue to arrange a

time and date. There are a few formalities: you will need to apply for a notice to marry no less than 15 days before you are due to wed and no more than a year in advance by taking a proof of identity and any documentation of previous marriages, as well as the details of where you are to marry to your local register office. You can also marry with very similar terms in a civil ceremony in Scotland.

Church of England

Thanks to a recent change in legislature, couples are now free to marry if either one of you has a connection to the parish in which you wish to wed (having either lived there for a period of over six months, been baptised in the parish or be living in the parish presently). Fees vary according to the diocese, but the wedding service is usually comprised of an hour long ceremony where you will be expected to say your vows in front of God, sing two or three hymns and attend a marriage preparation class to help you plan your wedding and understand more fully its significance - not as scary as it sounds, but a supportive session where you will look at the vows and assess your relationship. You will need to arrange for your 'banns' to be read on three Sundays over three months before the wedding at both the church you plan to marry in and your local parish church for a small fee – effectively your notice of marriage so you don't have to complete the paperwork as you would for a civil ceremony.

Church of Scotland

You can marry in any Church of Scotland venue with no residency required as long as it is conducted by an approved celebrant. You'll need to give notice 15 days before the wedding and no more than three months before your intended big day.

Catholic

A more devout ceremony full of lyrical readings and dazzling pomp. One of you will be expected to be baptised or prepared to be baptised to marry in a Catholic church. Marriage preparation courses are usually advised, and the ceremony itself includes mass with only biblical readings, and hymns.

Jewish

Traditionally held in a synagogue, you can also arrange to marry under a Chuppah (a special canopy lifted over the couple by loved ones) in other venues such as those listed for civil ceremonies and permanent marquees for an al-fresco style. Both bride and groom must be practising Jews or have converted to Judaism; the groom blesses the Torah a few days before the ceremony to show the couple's faithfulness to it when they marry, and both bride and groom will usually fast on the day of the wedding. The Jewish wedding ceremony is a traditional and joyous one, with the ritual smashing of the glass under the groom's heel usually resulting in jubilant cheers.

Other Faiths

Whether you are Muslim, Methodist, Sikh, Hindu, Baptist, URC, Orthodox, Buddhist, Taoist or Jehovah's Witness, most other marriage ceremonies are covered by a superintendent-registrar's certificate collected from the local registry office before the day to allow marriage in your chosen secular venue. See contact details for the General Register Office for England and Wales.

Humanist

A popular option for many, Humanism is a non-ecclesiastical philosophical movement that conducts wedding ceremonies – they are not legally recognised in England and Wales so you will need to undertake a civil ceremony beforehand (which you can do at little cost at a registry office). A Humanist ceremony is however recognised in Scotland.

Blessings

Most denominations and faiths will be happy to bless a civil marriage once the official part of the service is over, and it is a lovely way to nod to tradition or placate any parents who are religious. You are not tied to your local vicar, priest or celebrant so can choose any ordained minister you wish to bless you and your new spouse. Simply contact your chosen religious organisation and ask to be put in touch if you are not personally familiar with individuals who can perform such a blessing.

Insider Tip

"Think about any rules or sensitivities your denomination may have when looking for your wedding dress; for instance bare shoulders are sometimes frowned upon so you may need a lace jacket to cover up with for the ceremony".

Wedding Venues

Venue Hire Top Tips

1. For simplicity and to cut décor costs, look for a venue blessed with outstanding natural beauty that does all of the scene setting for you.

2. What means the most to you? Maybe it's a venue that encapsulates your favourite decade of style, or that allows for spaces with differing moods, or simply a venue big enough for all your guests and a mega-watt party. Go with your heart when it comes to finding a venue that fits the bill…

3. …And think outside the 'Saturday wedding' box. A weekday wedding offers considerably discounted rates so you can have the venue of your dreams (and if guests are given plenty of advanced warning, it gives them time to arrange an extra day's leave to attend the wedding of the year).

4. Though they allow you to put your own stamp on your wedding - often at winning rates - beware of the added costs of what we call a 'dry-hire' venue (a marquee or blank canvas space). Factor in heating, flooring, furniture, lighting, kitchen equipment for your catering team and lots of other hidden fees from toilet hire (sorry, the least glamorous part of wedding planning!) to PA systems for the speeches.

5. When haggling, do it with what we call a 'Marrakech' attitude: smile but be firm, respectful and polite. As a rule of thumb, start by negotiating at 2/3rds of what you are prepared to pay and work your way up (and include VAT). Always remember the English proverb 'Many things are lost from want of asking'!

6. One of the big bonuses of using a wedding planner (like us) is that our 'buying power' and the trust a venue places in us means we can negotiate preferential rates that we can pass on to you. We can also handle all of the 'un-seens' that come with any venue. This rings especially true when it comes to destination weddings.

7. There is no traditional 'wedding season' as such anymore but costs still vary with off-peak months such as September and May still at lower rates, although summer weddings are always at a premium (all that sunshine, gardens in full bloom and perfect wedding dress weather). If you're an autumn or winter lover, keen on mists, mellow fruitfulness or snowy winter wonderlands, ask for pictures of your venue or arrange a viewing at the right time of year so you get the full picture.

Here follows a selection of some of our most-loved wedding venues in the UK…

Nobu Berkeley ST Nobu London

Not content with being the hottest (and Michelin starred) restaurants to arrive on the London culinary scene in the past fifteen years, NOBU have branched out into weddings – and my, what a wedding venue these paens to discreet, but shimmering style NOBU London and NOBU Berkeley ST are. With its 'new style' Japanese menu suffused with peppy South American influences, from dishes of high-welfare Wagyu Beef Toban Yaki, feather-light Tempura Seafood, legendary Black Cod New York style with Miso the food here is an institution in its own right. Yet married as it is with interiors that are all refined, edgy glamour (thanks to design by the celebrated David Collins and United Designers collective respectively). The aesthetic at NOBU in the heart of Mayfair and the original NOBU just off Park Lane covering the entire first floor of design hotel, The Metropolitan, promises and delivers as impactful a wedding reception setting as you could wish for, featuring shimmering lacquered wood sushi bars.

Hosting anything up to 200 guests at NOBU Berkeley ST, featuring Hibachi lava-rock fire-bowl grills and Japanese wood-fired ovens all make for a spectacle-filled experience for your guests, too. Or with the option of more intimate wedding suppers in the suites and Private Dining Room of NOBU London, you can opt to wow your guests with their gastronomy almost anywhere with the new NOBU at Home catering service that spans full design and venue dressing - quite literally your own pop-up NOBU should you so wish – and catering for up to 400 guests.

Wrotham Park

Sink into a world of refinement:

300 acres of tranquil parkland in which is nestled this entirely lovely Palladian Mansion. Built in 1754 complete with neo-classical portico and corbels, it is easy to forget how close you are to central London (a mere 17 miles) and this is just one of the reasons why Wrotham Park makes for an such impeccable wedding venue. A rarity in that it is still in the hands of the family that commissioned its build, today it is all shimmering chandeliers and period charm.

Combining polished formality with the privacy of exclusive hire, the house is available on a limited number of occasions throughout the year. Although it does not hold a marriage licence, the appeal of Wrotham is in the chance to have your marriage blessed in the family chapel before an evening of dining and dancing. The rooms themselves are stately yet comfortable; we particularly like the romance of its duck-egg blue damask wallpaper and gilt flourishes. It is easy to envisage an adult wedding party here (the venue does not permit children due to the priceless artwork that adorns the walls), and the resulting wedding photographs which will echo the crisp grace of this special place.

And so to the food – the venue works with a select list of caterers that reflect its luxurious standards. Creating unique wedding breakfasts

to suit differing tastes and styles, these feasts are served on original banquet tables decked in beautiful ivory linen cloths and flickering candelabra; the setting positively glows. The only wonder is what secrets the walls could tell about the more lascivious speeches that have been given here over the years – or what antics its historic residents got up to in its smaller suites and enclaves, all of which are yours to explore.

Wrotham can accommodate up to 120 guests within the house, with larger parties spilling out onto a bespoke marquee abutting the house for a seamless feel. By allowing each wedding party to take over the estate entirely, Wrotham can be as individual as the bride and groom and there are many creative options for use of the space. Steps can be lined with storm lanterns and pretty foliage, dance floors can be constructed on the lawn - but the panoramic views over the surrounding countryside are what give this option that little something extra special. As a certain infamous show coined it, it's all about 'Location, Location, Location'.

Insider Tip

"Although overnight accommodation is not available within the house, there are a number of fabulous hotels close by we can recommend."

Castle Ashby

If you are looking for a wedding venue that basks in natural splendour, Castle Ashby is the place for you. Amid the 250 acres of Capability Brown parkland, ornamental gardens and water features sits a house that was built to entertain – Elizabeth I to be precise in 1574. It is a staggeringly handsome stately home to the 7th Marquess of Northampton, with classical porticos and loggia to the front which open out into a courtyard space. Everything here calls for an elegant wedding party from a bygone era: all punch bowls, thousands of candles and lots of dancing.

The mile-long avenue of leafy trees dates back to 1695; sweeping past them on your wedding day in a Landau carriage (what else), it is hard to not be carried away by the sense of pageantry and romance at Castle Ashby.

It is, however, the gardens that are the star attraction for a wedding here. Marry in the Great Hall or the charming parish church of St. Mary Magdalene before a wedding reception in one of the various 'secret garden' locations about the estate, Castle Ashby feels like a little dose of heaven, an arcadia on earth - what could be more romantic for a wedding day?

CEREMONIES

The Great Hall

With its oak wood panelling and historic portraits decking the walls, the Great Hall is a quintessentially grand room. A galleried hall that rises over two stories, you can perch a string quartet in the upper minstrel's gallery to announce the arrival of the bride with a brilliant fanfare. In later autumn months, the open fireplace can be dressed with armfuls of golden boughs, berries and candles to create a warm and radiant setting for your vows to be exchanged. Licensed for civil ceremonies, the Great Hall can seat up to 120 guests.

St Mary Magdalene Church

Tucked away in the grounds is this real hidden treasure - the quaint and very English church of St Mary Magdalene. Available for religious ceremonies or blessings with pews (and cushioned chairs) for 150 guests, it is airy by summer and cosy in cooler months.

RECEPTIONS

The North Lawn

With its panoramic views over the parkland, lakes and rolling countryside, the North Lawn blends garden party style with peaceful, idyllic nature. Graceful stone steps lead to a wonderful space for your marquee in which you can host the wedding breakfast and reception party of your dreams.

The East Terraces

From a lost era of promenades and wistfully British garden parties, the East Terraces are a light and pretty setting for an outdoor Champagne and canapé reception – perhaps with a touch of Great Gatsby-style jazz or a brass band covering 1940's classics. Frequently paired with the neighbouring North Lawn should you wish to spread your party to take in more of the heavenly gardens (who wouldn't?)

The Walled Garden

A real hideaway, this 16th century restored garden makes a winsome location for a secluded wedding party straight from the most romantic of English litrature (think Jane Austin or D H Lawrence). With ample space for larger weddings of up to 2,000 guests, it can be combined with the Italian Gardens if the weather is kind. It is a lovely setting for a deliciously long wedding lunch, with oodles of Champagne.

The Manor

The countryside wedding goes cool at this 13th century manor house. Set amid the undulating fields of Somerset under cornflower-blue skies with scudding cotton-wool clouds, The Manor is the quintessential idyll, having been transformed into a seriously stylish venue for weddings with a polished update.

From the outside, its pale honey stone walls, miniature lake and romantic manicured gardens make us think of enchanting wedding nuptials: but the clever twist at The Manor comes in the mix of sophisticated interiors and abundance of modern comforts. It offers the perfect wedding retreat, a hip hangout that will make any city dweller feel at home.

Maybe it's the outdoor heated pool or the Bvlgari toiletries, the opportunity to host a firework finale at your wedding reception or even the Michelin-quality fine dining from the French and English chefs, but there is something more than special about this place. If you're planning a wedding with country style and heaps of glamour, this is the venue for you. The oak-panelled Banquet Hall – with original inglenook fireplace and exposed beams – is an atmospheric and glorious backdrop for a civil ceremony for up to 60 seated guests (more standing). It's rendered particularly lovely and cosy in wintry months with a roaring log-fire, flickering lanterns and

boughs of evergreens. Alternatively, more intimate weddings can be held in the rustic Drawing Room for up to 20 seated guests.

There are many potential spaces for your reception. You can pitch an airy marquee for over 400 guests by the lake and deck it out with chandeliers and elegant furnishings in clear Perspex, crisp white and colour-pop flowers, or simply host a timeless feast in the Banquet Hall for 60 seated guests. The wedding breakfasts are one of the star attractions of a wedding here, and are sure to be a big hit with your guests. Every ingredient on the menu is locally sourced, with Chef Josh Eggleton (trained at one of America's finest restaurants, The French Laundry) creating innovative menus that include starters of blue cheese panna cotta with pear, walnut and squash salad, mains of Exmoor venison and Somerset apple Tarte Tatin with clotted ice-cream to finish. Followed by dancing till dawn, there is no-one to disturb your wedding for miles.

A wedding at The Manor is fully tailored to you, so whether you want to take over the entire house for the duration of a 'wedkend' with accommodation for up to 34 guests, or host your ceremony and reception here, you're free to be as indulgent as you like. This is the country house wedding venue but not as you know it.

Danesfield House

Just 45 minutes from London, this stunning white mock-Tudor country house hotel is packed with classic English charm. Nestled in the rolling green Chiltern Hills, there is something special about Danesfield House. Perhaps it is the incandescent light and how it streams into the house and lights up the high-ceilings and ornate fireplaces.

Or it could be the polished modernity of the Aromatherapy Associates Spa and the peaceful, immaculate gardens...

There are four settings for civil ceremonies to choose from; we particularly love the intimate Henley Room for up to 30 guests, swathed in sophisticated eau de nil and cream furnishings and boasting splendid bay windows, or the aptly named Versailles Suite, perfect for a grand wedding and holding up to 100 guests. Glittering crystal chandeliers, a multitude of mirrors and a touch of gold leaf on blush-peach walls certainly recreate a corner of the namesake palace in the heart of the Buckinghamshire countryside.

With just as many luxurious options for your reception, you can opt for an all-out lavish party from a bygone era. Hold a wedding feast set on the banqueting table in the Versailles suite following a drinks reception on the south facing terrace, or a garden party for up to 250 guests in the elegant glass-sided marquee. Why not take over the house in its entirety and cosy up with your guests on the evening before your wedding, then collapse into a downy four-poster bed for that all-important beauty sleep. There is ample accommodation for guests to unwind, so you can relax in the knowledge everyone will be comfortable and will never want to leave.

Michelin-starred chef Adam Simmonds inspired the seasonal wedding breakfast menus, from slow-roast beef sirloin topped with horseradish purée and earthy girolle mushrooms, to delightful puddings of treacle tart or pistachio crème brulée. Danesfield offers everything there is to love about a country house wedding, wrapped in a luxurious hotel package.

The Dorchester

Decisions, decisions!

Two venues both alike in sensational style and grace: Dorchester Collection's London Grande Dame and first country house hotel and spa, Coworth Park, make for two show-stopping settings whatever your wedding style.

With its rarefied, original 1930s aesthetic and prime Hyde Park location shouldered by shady horse chestnut trees, Italianate fountains and magenta flowers, where better to play out your most glamorous wedding fantasies than The Dorchester? Blending polished marble floors, a recently renovated vast ballroom with its own private entrance off Park Lane and just the right dose of Art Deco elegance, don't let the shimmering vintage details fool you. It is equally possessed of a contemporary, light touch that makes it perfect for a town wedding of anything up to 500 guests, and is the only ballroom venue in London offering à la carte dining.

There are eight striking banqueting suites licensed for civil ceremonies; we adore the pistachio green and fresco detailing of The Pavilion, or the circular Gold Room with its painted-cloud ceiling and rococo romance. Yet, could there be a more exquisite setting than The Ballroom with its beautiful backdrop of gold, sky blue and crisp white? Perfect for more intimate affairs or grand receptions, The Dorchester wedding experience is as luxurious as they come. With in-house floristry, hair stylists and one of the best spas in the city, there's even complimentary wedding night accommodation. Everything here is designed for the most grown-up and glittering celebration of your life.

Coworth Park

If you are happiest in the verdant countryside and dream of a wedding that blends rural romance with the Dorchester Collection's legendary style, Coworth Park is the venue for you. Surrounded by wildflower meadows and Windsor Great Park yet a mere 45 minutes from London, the setting is quite simply idyllic. This glorious Georgian mansion is hidden among 240 acres of the prettiest and most tranquil parkland, dotted with oak trees and a lime grove. While Coworth Park is every inch the perfect country wedding venue, The Dorchester's refinement most definitely translates to the country. The antithesis of the chintzy country hotel when it comes to cool, Coworth's lovely five-star facilities include an eco-spa and with comfortable, understated interiors in a muted palette of honey, cotton white and copper. There's a nod to the surroundings with a sculptural wreath of bronze leaves circling above the dining tables of the Restaurant Coworth Park, and four-poster beds featuring branch-like details for a fabulous bucolic touch.

You can marry in one of the four licensed events spaces, before hosting an al fresco reception for anything up to 250 guests in the semi-permanent marquee. Just imagine sitting outside feasting on the most delicious, locally-sourced food with all of your family and friends, the hurricane lanterns twinkling as dusk falls. We love Coworth Park for its modern take on the dream country wedding, and strongly suspect you will, too.

No.4 Hamilton Place

With its perfect Park Lane location and inimitable Edwardian style, No.4 Hamilton Place is elegance itself. This beautiful town house built in 1907 is as close to a stately home in London as you are bound to come; for a luxurious and super stylish statement wedding venue, this is a firm favourite.

No.4 Hamilton Place exemplifies everything we love about crisp English grandeur, with its grand edifice perhaps only surpassed by the impeccable personal service within. It really is a case of 'what's mine is yours' and you can take over the entire lovingly maintained house exclusively. With its sweeping views across Hyde Park from the arched sash windows, or spread across the eight spaces including the private, heated terrace for cocktails and gourmet BBQ at sunset in the summer months, it's easy to see the appeal of hosting your wedding here. The delicate update on its Louis XIV interior (inspired by the Ritz hotel of 1906) is a showcase for the details; fine cornicing, open fireplaces, ochre damask wallpaper and the filigreed banisters of the central staircase with its antique chandelier. Even the ladies' powder room warrants a mention for its pretty crimson Toile de Jouy wallpaper and period drama polish.

The award-winning food fuses modern freshness full of organic, free range and artisan ingredients sourced from the best of British producers.

A wedding breakfast menu can include canapés of wild mushroom palmiers with Welsh goats' cheese and slow roast tomatoes, beetroot cured gravadlax with charred asparagus and lemon balm salad for starters, followed by braised beef cheek, onions, pancetta and smoked garlic pomme purée or even authentic Spanish tapas before finishing with a cherry and chocolate tartine.

You can marry in a civil ceremony or partnership in one of three licensed settings about the house; each of which is graced with the characteristic warmth and quiet splendour of No. 4 Hamilton Place. Accommodating up to 200 guests, your reception can be centred on one of the larger salons or you can create distinct feels in enclaves about the house with the stylish use of floristry, varied live music, food and furnishings. Channelling everything we love about sumptuous Parisian supper clubs, the Argyll room looks particularly opulent dressed in heavy red velvet and towering brass candlesticks to match its swagged curtains and gold trimmed plaster relief work. Equally, this room can be transformed into a pure vision of romance with white-washed chairs and a muted palette of dusky blue hydrangeas and chic grey accents. Whichever you choose, add the modern finishing touches of air-conditioned rooms, sophisticated sound systems and the delicious food, and you have a winning setting for a wedding that's as chic as they come in Mayfair.

Stapleford Park

One of those beautiful English stately homes we do so well, Stapleford Park Country House Hotel and Sporting Estate is a wedding venue that is at once irrefutably impressive, but wonderfully relaxed and welcoming too. There is no fustiness or 'don't touch the china' etiquette here, which lends Stapleford Park a charming and homely atmosphere which comes into its own if you take over the house exclusively and play Lord and Lady of the Manor. You could even indulge in some country pursuits of falconry, archery, shooting and horse riding over a wedding weekend for some real great Country House and hunt parties from a bygone age.

Set in a tableau of gently rolling grounds, the largely 17th century manor house takes pride in its location set among a 500 acre estate. Everything here blends country refinement from the vast windows which allow pools of pale golden light to flood the house for a serene ambiance, to the antique antlers adorning the walls. It is also incredibly peaceful, with birdsong and startlingly clear night skies offering a stunning backdrop for photographs and a home-from-home escape. It is little wonder Stapleford Park was recently voted one of Britain's top 50 wedding venues, and is a go-to favourite for high profile and celebrity nuptials.

Stapleford Park is certainly perfect for weddings when it comes to romance. From the exterior you could even be mistaken for thinking yourself in France, such is the château-like elegance of the pale stone façade framed by a sweeping

gravel drive and box hedge gardens. The lovely Orangery suits a larger wedding ceremony, and is licensed for civil ceremonies with up to 150 guests. Throwing open the doors, why not host your Champagne and canapé reception in one of the many manicured gardens? You can even have your marriage blessed in the sweet St Mary Magdalene church in the grounds before a short walk to your wedding breakfast in the Grand Hall. With its glittering crystal chandeliers and pale blue colour scheme, the hall is just one of the gorgeous rooms scattered throughout the house you can use and seats up to 180 guests. More intimate wedding receptions are held in the Harborough room (named for one of the noble families that once owned Stapleford Park) whose walls are decorated in Gainsboroughs. It is all distinctive, stylish, and charmingly refined.

The wedding breakfast is a revelation, with seasonal, locally sourced and delicious dishes such as guinea fowl with stuffed confit leg,

Savoy cabbage and fondant potato. The wine cellar is well stocked with some of the worlds finest; you would hardly know which one to choose. Wedding parties are accommodated in the 48 bedrooms of the house, which are each individually styled by quintessentially British designers including Mulberry's Emma Hill, Nina Campbell and David Hicks. You could even arrive early for some big day preparation at the Clarins Gold Spa housed in the converted stable block, or relax in the pool, steam room and Jacuzzi located in the Main House. Grooms and their friends will also no doubt be tempted to unwind at the 18 hole championship golf course that Stapleford Park is also renowned for.

Stationery Guide

Smythson

There is nothing lovelier than a good quality, properly presented invitation to a wedding. This is not a time for gimmicks or emails, but for something more meaningful and beautiful to behold. For 125 years, Smythson have been purveyors of the most luxurious handmade stationery; a fine tradition they continue to this day. From the crisp tradition of hand-milled, watermarked and die-stamped cards, (thick, velvety textured papers with engraving to me and you) to modern twists of design and wording or little personalised nuances, Smythson takes the details seriously.

Smythson's Bespoke Stationery service is what really sets them apart. Under their trained experts' diligent, individual care they will help you create a suite of wedding stationery that expresses your tastes and fits your wedding's aesthetic, whether it be rock n' roll, contemporary or classically elegant. After all, this is the equivalent of you hand writing to each and every one of your dear ones to make them feel special.

Wedding stationery should mark the event as the once-in-a-lifetime occasion it is and this means you should not scrimp on its appearance, spirit or sense of fun. What makes Smythson so special (and our ultimate destination for stationery) is their unique ability to blend a signature respect for tradition founded on generations of experience,

and a trend-led lightness of touch. Die-stamped, intense ink pigments and a host of delicate tissues, cards, ribbons and gilded lettering all come together to deliver the finest quality finished products. The die-stamping process is revered for its ability to produce delicate lines and the trademark 'bruising' that gently shows as a mark of quality on the reverse. Smythson are certainly masters of it.

Guiding you through each stage of the process from Save the Date to Thank-You cards, here is the essential guide to Smythson Bespoke Stationery...

Save the Date Cards

Save the Date cards are crucial when it comes to setting the tone as they are the first hint that many of your guests will have of your wedding's style and mood. They build the initial flurry of anticipation, and should linger in guests' minds as a date they simply cannot miss. Save the Date cards are also increasingly popular as a way of booking your day into busy diaries. As a rule of thumb, they should be sent out six months in advance of your wedding day. If you are marrying abroad, on a Bank Holiday weekend or at any other time that is likely to prove busy for many, you may want to send Save the Date cards out earlier to allow for the booking of hotels and flights. It is also a little forewarning for any avid sports fans you may be thinking of inviting who

can't decide whether it's your wedding day or the World Cup that they want to make (and if it's the latter, consider them firmly struck off the guest list).

It is essential that they convey the details of 'who' is getting married, 'when' and 'where.' 'Where' can be approximate such as the county or country if you do not have a firm venue booked, or if you wish to keep things a little mysterious to build intrigue. Other than these particulars, you can be as imaginative as you like. Most couples work backwards from their invitation to decide upon the style of each component of their stationery. The Save the Date cards often reflect the invitation in a lighter, simplified version using the same papers or ink colours.

Mr. and Mrs Mark Harrison ❶

request the pleasure of your company

at the marriage of their daughter ❷

Daniella Claire

to

Mr. Philip Edward Sykes

at St. George's Church, Hanover Square ❸

on Saturday 1ˢᵗ May 2011

at 2 o'clock

and afterwards at

The Langham

RSVP ❹
104 Paradise Walk
London SW3 4HP

Invitations

The invitation gives your guests all relevant details of the wedding day, in addition to being a thing of beauty. Traditionally, invitations are sent out six to eight weeks prior to the big day. Stationery styles shift like fashion trends, but the appeal of hand-milled, understated stationery is timeless. There are lots of decisions to be made - do you opt for a pure text invitation written in twinkling metallic ink, or a card adorned with an image symbolic for you?

Whilst Smythson specialise in engraving, you can liven up the classic invite with their collection of 14 coloured cards with 32 hues of tissue, or hand-painted borders and motifs. Typography can be as exuberant or pared-back as you like. It is however essential that it is legible, as you do not want guests to arrive at the wrong venue due to an over-enthusiastic flourish of calligraphy.

When it comes to wording, check with the wishes of the host, although as weddings are increasingly paid for by the couple, formalities can often be loosened. The template above is an example of what you will need to include, with the conventional wording, covering 'who', 'what' (whether the guest is invited to the ceremony, wedding breakfast or the evening reception only),'where' and 'when.'

The Extras

Alongside your invitation, you may wish to include fuller details of the day and any particular information that will make both you and your guests' lives easier during what is sure to be a hugely busy time leading up to the wedding. These can be printed on fine paper or a card in contrasting or matching hues, or as part of a booklet for a seamless feel to complement your stationery (and to help guests keep all the sheets together). Smythson would suggest you include the following items as necessities in your inserted sheets:

- Prepare information sheets detailing the precise location of the ceremony and reception venues. Include any local landmarks that may assist your guests if the venue is tricky to find, or if Sat-Nav is likely to flounder.
- A map can also be helpful: even better if it is a hand-drawn one with hotels, pubs, and other note-worthy distractions included. This can be especially useful if you have a situation in which you are inviting guests to the reception only, as you can suggest beauty spots, activities or restaurants to be sampled - and lose some of the guilt in the process.
- Include information on childcare (whether you are supplying it or recommending local crèches or nannies).
- Make it clear if transport has been arranged for guests between the ceremony venue and reception, or include the telephone numbers of local taxi firms and locations of car parks to help guests as much as possible if they are making their own way.
- If you are marrying abroad, supply the booking details of key flight providers and your hand-picked local hotels.
- Ask for the particulars of any dietary requirements to avoid hungry guests at the wedding because they have not been adequately catered for.
- Although British wedding etiquette does not require a dress code (we love any excuse to dress up) you may wish to specify what the bride and groom parties will be wearing such as lounge suit or morning suit to act as a guide for guests.

RSVP Cards

Purists tend to prefer hand-written notes of acceptance, but including RSVP cards makes it easier for guests to reply promptly as they are not hunting around for cards or the time to write such a missive. A double-sided postcard is a good option here, with stamp included for ease.

Gift List

This can be intertwined with the information sheet or it can simply be a postcard with the web address and gift list register details such as your names or the account name. Many gift list companies supply these as part of their service.

Orders of Service

These can simply be the credits of the readings, music and the names of the wedding party, or richer documents for guests to take away and cherish. A booklet of watermarked card with leaves of sheer paper makes a pretty impression.

Menus

A stylish card elaborating on your chosen breakfast will whet appetites and can be a good conversation starter. Mention how the pudding choice stems from your Great-Auntie Maggie or, perhaps, where you first tasted the starter.

Thank You Notelets

Always express your gratitude to the guests who have shared in your day and been so generous with their gifts. Smythson make some delicious little correspondence cards on which you can have an image from your wedding printed. It is also an opportune moment for the bride to use her newly married name.

We love the idea of ordering a whole ream of personalised stationery with your married names emblazoned across the set. Handy for any occasion including invitations to sample the results of the cocktail making set you received from your wedding list, or to send news and photos to those who could not attend your wedding.

Leather Stationery

Wedding planners don't come more chic than Smythson's little tome. It is the perfect place to log your favourite tip-offs, receipts and suppliers in Dress, Invitations, Guests and Gifts, Service, Reception, Flowers and Other, Going Away and Honeymoon indexes.

Guest Book

Keep a poignant memento of your day with an embossed leather guest book: ask your guests to record their impressions of your wedding day, any fond memories and anecdotes of you as a couple. You will cherish it forever.

Passport Covers

Discreet, beautiful and the perfect opportunity to herald your marriage: grooms and brides should have their spouse's name gold-stamped on one of these stylish wallets.

Photo Albums and Frames

Inscribe a line from your vows onto a soft leather photo album that contains your favourite pictures from the wedding. Even better, opt for a travel frame so that you can reminisce wherever the winds blow you.

JULIAN AND NATALIE SURTEES
25 GLOUCESTER CRESCENT
25 GLOUCESTER CRESCENT, LONDON SW1 3PB
020 7352 5267   julian@nataliesurtees.com

25 GLOUCESTER CRESCENT
LONDON SW1 3PB

JULIAN SURTEES

90 654321   julian@nataliesurtees.com

SMYTHSO

EST 1887

OF BOND STREET

Insider Tip

By ordering all of your stationery at the same time,
you may be able to reduce print and delivery costs
while also ticking stationery off your wedding
planning list in one fell swoop.

Wedding Floristry

Absolute Flowers & Home

Say hello to what must surely be one of the prettiest and most pleasurable aspects of wedding planning: the flowers!

Ever since the doors of her beautiful shop opened in 1999, Hayley Newstead's Absolute Flowers & Home have been our go-to boutique for wedding floristry. Marrying modern luxury with just the right amount of thoroughbred romance they are feted for their style-setting way with blooms. The highly skilled team are known for their glamorously sensual aesthetic. Leading the way in wow-factor flowers from their Little Venice studio, Absolute's floristry is loved by the likes of Vogue and Tatler, with the loyal, starry clientele to match.

Blending perfectly pitched enhancements to any venue with striking individuality, theirs is a truly personal approach. Absolute proves that wedding floristry can be fresh, modern and chintz-free with high-octane, flawless arrangements and bouquets. Sculpted and preened into naturally breath taking décor, each arrangement features lashings of the finest quality flowers in the world.

Whether you choose to keep things soft and sophisticated with sweet powder-scented garden flowers, or have your heart set on heady bacchanalia, the passionate team at Absolute will match the wedding style you have set your heart on with astonishing floristry.

Read on as Absolute Flowers & Home's Founder, Hayley Newstead, shares expert tips and the golden rules of wedding flowers…

GETTING STARTED

We always advise brides to start planning wedding floristry three to four months before the big day; although it is always a good idea to pencil in your wedding with your florist up to a year in advance, as many become especially busy over peak wedding season.

Tackle the focal points with our guide to the essentials overleaf, and concentrate on the arrangements with the most impact to maximise your budget.

ABSOLUTE FLOWERS & HOME'S GUIDE TO WEDDING FLOWERS

Bouquets

Ranging from oh-so-pretty posies and pomanders to teardrops or ball bouquets, there is one to match every budget and style. Here at Absolute we feel less is more – flowers are already so beautiful that sometimes it is best to leave Mother Nature to wow. Above all, a bouquet has to compliment the brides gown, not overpower. Opt for wired or hand-tied bouquets for a more structured, elegant look or looser, country feel respectively. However, wired bouquets are time-consuming work so be sure to allow for the additional cost. Including fragrant flowers is a lovely touch; heighten the sensory allure with a spritz of your favourite perfume.

Bridesmaids Bouquets

These are usually smaller, more economical versions of the bride's bouquet. Complementing the whole colour scheme by picking up the shades of the bridesmaids dresses or vice versa, the dresses will play a part in choosing the proportions and style of the bouquets. Whether you echo bridesmaids dresses with softer flowers in a generous bunch or small hits of vivid colour, creating a seamless look is a must.

Flower Girl

Adorable and delicate circlet crowns of flowers look lovely on little bridemaids.

Buttonholes

Traditionally a buttonhole was a small bunch of foliage and greenery, but how about adding interest by picking out blooms from the bride's bouquet. Worn by the groom, father of the bride and all male members of the wedding party (best man and ushers), the groom's should have that little something extra that marks him out as special.

Corsages

These are slightly larger versions of buttonholes worn by the Mother of the Bride and Groom. Be careful when pinning corsages onto dresses as they can cause the dress to tug down, but they look pretty as bracelets or pinned to hats and bags.

Table Arrangements

For stunning centrepieces, why not use different designs and heights? When guests walk into the room, they will be captivated by the layers of detail. Try setting some tables with solid arrangements centred on tall candelabras, scattered vases of varying heights or creating a living table runner with an array of blooms. Guests spend the greatest proportion of the day at the reception, therefore table arrangements should be given lots of thought and make for a large part of your floristry budget.

Swags, Wreaths & Garlands

Although quite a traditional way to decorate doorways and fireplaces, these can be brought up-to-date using abundant tonal flowers. This looks particularly lovely in churches at the end of pews and also on the corners of a Huppah.

Decorative Arrangements

Positioned in windowsills, stairwells or dotted around a venue; you can brighten or create individual feels in spaces with generous arrangements of flowers in urns or containers set upon pillars.

THE SEVEN KEY INGREDIENTS TO BEAUTIFUL WEDDING BLOOMS

1. Dream

Tear and collect images of flowers, interiors, fashion and things you love from magazines and blogs to give an idea of your wedding's style. Your florist will then create moodboards and designs of how your flowers could look.

2. Budget

Do not leave budgeting for your flowers till last; ask your florist for a quote first. Take into consideration delivery, installation and labour costs as a lot of time and love will go into your wedding flowers.

3. Think Venue

Many venues already have beautiful fixtures and furnishings so lavish arrangements never fail to set them off to their best advantage. Starker, blank canvas venues (such as marquees or crisp white spaces) look lovely with simple floristry, whilst you can also add colour and texture for a romantic mood. Identify the focal points of your venue, and let your florist add the requisite oomph.

4. Colour me Pretty

Choose a palette sympathetic to your venue and dress; but do not be afraid of a colourful, fashion-forward scheme. You can always play with the balance until it's absolutely perfect.

5. Think Differently

No two weddings are ever the same, so do not feel limited by conventional floristry. Make your mark with flowers that reflect your personal style and tastes.

6. Romance

Embrace it! Weddings are the ultimate dose of romance, so why not go classic by using a classic bloom such as roses. Neutral tones of blush, cream and white are Absolute's signature; these are shades that will never date, and are eternally chic.

7. TLC

Your wedding flowers should be treated with the utmost love and care. Source them from the best possible supplier, and ensure all measures are taken to maintain the flower so they are in perfect condition and full bloom on your big day.

WHAT'S IN, WHEN?

Whilst many flowers from perennial favourites such as Lily of the Valley to English garden roses can be sourced year round. If you love a particular seasonal variety or have a unique look in mind, why not set your wedding date for when your chosen flowers will be at their best?

Spring

Think tulips, hyacinths, muscari, snowbells, and paperwhites for a whimsical and pretty feel; or an abundance of cherry blossom for delicate texture.

Summer

Garden flowers abound, with hydrangeas at their best and resplendent scented blooms from garden roses to peonies.

Autumn

Simply add twinkling candles and armfuls of velvety blooms to create a warm and rich feel.

Winter

Lots of reflective, sparkling vases and accessories will make a winter wedding feel festive and magical.

Feasting

The Wedding Feast *from Caroline Hurley*

Here is our essential guide

to wedding breakfasts, cake and delectable edibles from Caroline Hurley.

When it comes to the meal of a lifetime – for that is what a wedding breakfast most definitely is, always think with your tummy. This is your chance to dazzle guests with not only your impeccable taste, but indulge in your favourite treats with a menu that nods to your travels, comfort foods, family heirloom recipes and memorable meals shared over the course of your romance. Caterers increasingly offer personalised menus filled with a plethora of artisan goodies, and are giving the traditional sit-down wedding feast a shake-up with original ways of serving and classics made brand new. Whether you are planning a formal dinner of three courses or more, or a casual yet elegant supper, these are my key ingredients for delicious feasting food to savour...

THE BASICS

Canapés

A morsel that can be eaten in one bite (or two delicate ones); whilst France claims to have invented them, miniature versions of English classics are just as scrumptious. Think potted shrimp with brioche toast, foie gras doughnuts, and truffled cheese on toast.

Wedding Breakfast

Usually a sit-down meal with waitress service, this was traditionally served after the wedding ceremony (which was held early in the morning, hence 'breakfast') and usually features a handful of courses, some of which may have multiple entrée options. Always allow for adequate staff to cater to guests, and take note of dietary requirements via your invitations, asking for preferred meal choices (vegetarian, vegan, coeliac etc.) and intolerances to make serving easy.

Wedding Buffet

More relaxed in style, host a BBQ with outdoor dining and gourmet cuts of meat such as filet mignon served with triple-cooked chips, or recreate a street food feel with stations of sushi, gourmet hot dogs, oyster barrows and lobster roll bars. Sharing plates of tapas or meats with elegant salads in bowls on the table also create a warm, friendly atmosphere that breaks the ice as guests pass dishes around.

Cake

Layered confections featuring different flavours of iced sponge; the tiers of a wedding cake are (according to folklore) inspired by the fanciful steeple of St. Bride's church in London built in 1701 – 1703. It is sometime served in place of dessert or as a favour, and can be made from smaller cakes such as cupcakes and macaroons in towers, too.

Midnight Munchies

Serve a late-evening supper of snacks and light food to keep your guests going and tummies lined.

Tea Party

Host a quintessentially English tea party in the late afternoon replete with wicker furnishings or picnic-style with baskets of clotted cream scones, goats' cheese tartlets, and infused Champagne cocktails in addition to good old fashioned tea.

Cocktails

Commission your bartender to whip up a signature cocktail for you, and make like old high society by holding a cocktail hour with lounge music.

GOLDEN RULES

Wedding planners abide by one golden rule: if you get the food, cake and fizz right the rest will follow. And always over-cater – hungry guests will inevitably become sloshed and rowdy.

Buy local, seasonal and high-welfare wherever you can for a menu that cares. This also lends your meal an authenticity and a greater chance your guests will never have tasted dishes before so your wedding is guaranteed to stand out in their memory.

Allocate two thirds of a bottle of wine to every adult guest to accompany their wedding breakfast, a fifth of a bottle of Champagne for toasts and do not forget plenty of water and soft drinks.

DID YOU KNOW?

The word 'honeymoon' is derived from the Irish tradition of the drinking of mead at the wedding celebrations and also the newlyweds sipping a cup of mead every evening for the duration of the lunar cycle after they marry. A nice modern interpretation is to use a little honey in your wedding breakfast or in your favours, such as honey fudge or little jars of honey with 'Love is Sweet' labels.

Over the following pages I would like to introduce you to some of Quintessentially Weddings' avourite caterers and cake bakers...

"rhubarb"

With generous wedding

breakfasts made from fresh, sun-filled ingredients or feasts of toasty Englishness, "rhubarb" is a wedding caterer we cannot resist. When it comes to turning an ordinary wedding into something quite fantastical, food needs to be remarkable on all counts and the talented team behind Lucy Gemmell's "rhubarb" (established in 1996) certainly come up trumps. It was the classic gruyère soufflés with warm asparagus and Noilly Prat creamed sauce that first got us hooked; in fact, everything the team touches will make your guests remember your glorious wedding for a long time to come.

Elegant sit-down dinners, cosmopolitan blends of Pan Asian or authentic Indian dishes – whatever your choice, each menu can cater to a variety of set-ups, venues, styles and budget. This is genuinely personal catering that encompasses all of the things that you would treat yourself to (triple cooked chips cooked in duck fat for example). Provenance and respect for the seasonality of food is of prime concern to "rhubarb". Each dish allows the ingredients to shine, thanks to exquisite presentation and innovative techniques - notably in collaboration with Heston Blumenthal.

Traditionally, a wedding breakfast consists of canapés and a Champagne reception followed by a three or four course meal with your cake, then plenty of cocktails and dancing stoked by a light supper. You could easily devise a menu from their canapé list alone, so enticing is the list: foie gras mousse coated in hazelnut butter, topped with toasted hazelnuts and fragments of honeycomb; lobster toasts topped with lemongrass and sweet chilli, Cumberland sausages with creamed shallot-scented potato mousseline and deep fried oysters in salted kombu with a citrus dashi vapour. There is also mouth-watering tortellini with summer squash, fontina cheese, date and orange purée, toasted almonds and beurre-noisette, Ragstone goats' cheese soufflé with roasted chestnuts and figs, or Cumbrian Lamb with 'The Forgotten Allotment' of summer vegetables and a lamb tea jus served in sweet little teapots. Puddings range from rhubarb and strawberry cobbler with rose petal ice-cream, Black Forest fondants with mulled cherries and Kirsch, Eton Mess, blackcurrant sorbet or in winter, pistachio brulée with chocolate crackle and chestnut Mont Blanc. Yum!

Served by charming and unstuffy staff, everything comes together to make for a seamless wedding feast. Mixologist's can whip up a mean personlised drink for you, and sommeliers can help select wines to breathe life into your menu. Book them anything up to a year in advance to avoid disappointment, and ensure the bride's dress has an extra inch or two of give in it; you won't want to miss out on one single mouthful.

Absolute Taste

With a penchant for sophisticated, chic and modern flavours, Absolute Taste undoubtedly wow anyone lucky enough to sample their food. Established in 1997 with Ron Dennis and Lyndy Redding at the helm, they supply passionately prepared wedding catering at its best, using top quality local and seasonal ingredients. We're as equally impressed with their striking food inspired by Lyndy's travels as we are their slick global catering operation. Menus feature

artisan touches and great British food, but the close-knit team are dab hands at fusion cuisine, sushi and have a mean way with a cocktail, too. You can also depend on them for the finest wines, saving yourself time and corkage fees as experienced sommeliers match the most appropriate labels to your wedding menu.

Absolute Taste offer a fully bespoke service to suit your big day, be it a traditional wedding breakfast or a more relaxed affair with stalls of Gourmet street food. One thing's for sure, the company's level of creativity ensures that no two weddings will ever be the same.

From canapés of tiny new season Spring lamb skewers crusted in mint and pine nut with delicate fresh lavender, redcurrant glaze and a minty pesto dip, to posh chunky chips with fresh truffle dipping sauce or baby brioche filled with wild cèpes and lemon hollandaise – all so tempting that you'll be hard pushed to keep some room even for the main course. Starters of Scottish lobster ravioli or ham hock and walnut terrine with Chardonnay pickled onions pave the way for signature roast Aberdeen Angus beef with horseradish rosti, or slow-roasted Gloucestershire old spot pork belly with a sweet honey glaze, thyme infused potato Dauphinoise, crackling sausage roll and cute kilner jars of spiced apple and caramelised red onion jam. Just make sure you don't miss the puddings: chocolate and ginger truffle tarts, apple trifle with cider granite and cinnamon doughnut, or the prettiest elderflower and gold leaf jellies served in miniature glasses for added twinkle.

Insider Tip
"Why not host a traditional High Tea in place of a canapé reception, with cocktails served in vintage tea cups and saucers, baby scones with Cornish clotted cream and local strawberries for a refreshing and elegant twist"

the-recipe

Why do we love the-recipe?

Not just for their seriously talented team (one of whom, Ash Mair has recently gone on to win Masterchef Professional), or the sense of celebratory occasion they bring to every wedding with their delectable food. Oh no, they are a regular fixture at many of our events and weddings in particular because of their creative and meticulous approach to every commission that ensures your nuptials are utterly memorable.

the-recipe blends all of the best bits of feel-good British food with innovative twists gleaned from an exhaustive knowledge of the London gastronomic scene. Their regular research visits to the latest eateries give them that 'foodie caterer's' edge. They have worked with the likes of Marc Jacobs, Vogue, Calvin Klein and even the Observer Food Monthly Awards – a strong indication of how very good they are.

Whatever the venue or style, the-recipe will meticulously plan a menu that brings all of your favourite foods and flavours together. You can go for a pop-up restaurant feel or a formal sit down breakfast of manifold courses. Attended by attentive and professional staff, the whole operation is very slick indeed. Their cocktails and wine lists are to die for, with some of London's top bartenders frequently making an appearance behind the bar to shake up mixes and bespoke drinks if you want to put your own stamp on the fun.

Allow us to rave about the dishes the-recipe can create for one moment: imagine your Champagne reception with little bites of heaven in the form of Ash goats' cheese on brioche toast with roasted pear and truffled honey (certain to cause a stampede) or a breakfast that includes a duo of lamb; herb crusted cannon and slow-roasted shoulder with butternut squash purée, turnip fondant and glazed cippolini onions. Don't even get us started on the puddings - rosemary panna cotta, wild berry jelly and Champagne granite to name just one.

Laurent-Perrier

Nothing says 'wedding' quite like free-flowing Champagne; a pale gold effervescent fluid that legend has it is here by chance. Created by one André-Michel Pierlot, this Champagne House established in 1812 has grown to become one of the largest family-run and most prestigious Champagne producers in the gilded Épernay region. Named for its second and third generation owners Eugène Laurent and his widow Mathilde-Emilie Perrier, every bottle from this artful house is still guided by the philosophy of integrity, innovation and quality that its founders so cherished. Taking the best Chardonnay, Pinot Noir and Pinot Meunier grapes and a unique yet natural second fermentation process for those definitive bubbles, there are now seven Champagnes from the Laurent-Perrier house each as lovely as the next; and the perfect way in which to toast the start of a very happy marriage.

Insider Tips

1. "If you buy your Champagne a while before the wedding to lay it down, rest the Champagne gently on its side to allow the cork to remain damp and plump; thus preventing air from creeping in and ruining the taste."

2. "Try to avoid opening your Champagne until the very last minute to retain as much fizz as possible. Chill at an ambient temperature of around 10°C — two to three hours max should do the trick."

Little Venice Cake Company

At the heart of the wedding
feast sits the wedding cake; a once-in-a-lifetime
creation of sugar-laced loveliness to be snaffled at
the end of the wedding breakfast, or miniature cakes
carried away as keepsakes. They certainly don't come
much more delectable nor beautiful than those of
Mich Turner (MBE) and her cohorts at Little Venice
Cake Company in our opinion.

Mich has notched up almost twenty five years as
a cake maker, producing joyously pretty cakes
for the likes of the Queen and a host of stars - a
testament to her high-spec knowledge and stylish
touch. You can even have a bash at recreating
some of the cakes yourself with the help of one of
Mich's award winning books, or by going behind
the scenes on a cake masterclass.

From the star-dusted Couture Rock and Rose
cake to the delicate Crown Can-Can cakes with
their frilly chocolate tops or Versailles Birds,
(inspired by Matthew Williamson), each cake is not
just your traditional ivory three-tiered affair, but the
high-octane, glamourous version. The best part? The
contents hidden inside these fabulous hand-piped
sugar facades. Light as air sponges with lemon or
Madagascan Vanilla, luscious truffle tortes made
with Callebaut chocolate and the Queen Elizabeth
Date Cake with exotic sticky medjool dates, apple,
ginger and fresh lemon: every cake is bespoke and
a little bit of heaven.

Insider Tips
From Mich Turner

*1. "Don't feel limited by notions of what's right
– choose a wedding cake that reflects your
personality."*

*2. "You may wish to preserve the top fruit cake
tier to celebrate the birth of your firstborn, as is
traditional."*

Rosalind Miller

With ravishing style and a
delicate sweetness, a Rosalind Miller wedding cake
would surely have been worthy of Marie-Antoinette
in her day. Forget the traditional identikit and
multi-tiered traditional affair; every cake created
by Rosalind is one-of-a-kind with surface detailing
in icing and ganache that would be the envy of a
couturier. Her background as an artist and designer
shines through in each of her creations, all of which
are truly edible works of art. Delicate towers in
muted pastel shades or edible gold leaf are adorned
with cut-out filigree lace work, frills that look as

if they were made from tulle, blossoms and birds.
Needless to say, the cakes are delectable and
range from Sicilian lemon with homemade lemon
curd filling, subtle floral-inspired flavours such as
lavender and rose vaguely reminiscent of Turkish
delight, to rhubarb or raspberry, and the staple
Madagascan vanilla and Belgian chocolate sponges
with matching buttercreams. Established in 2010 as
an extension of Rosalind's feted 'Peggy's Cupcakes',
her wedding cakes have graced society weddings,
the pages of national bridal magazines, fashion
magazines and television.

Cakes by Krishanthi

Hand-painted birdcage motifs, whirls of white-piped icing and some of the most delicate yet seductive ingredients in town; Krishanthi Armitt's wedding cakes are pure fantasy. When it comes to the centrepiece of your wedding feast, look no further. Design-led and distinctive, she turns a talent for baking and rigorous formal sugar-craft training to producing some of the most artful wedding cakes we've seen. Every cake is handmade to commission using organic, Fairtrade and free-range ingredients to ensure quality and taste. It's partly the flavours - be it mocha espresso coffee, or almond infused sponge cake with clementine syrup - but the decoration is the star attraction.

GC Couture

Soft pink petals, lace and gilded ornamentation mark GC Couture's wedding cakes out as statements of luxury. Rightly famed for their glamorous creations that encase 41 flavoured sponges, each puts a delectable spin on the conventional with fruitcakes-without-the-bits or white chocolate laced with perky ginger. Inspired by 20th century design, the cakes range from a white-lustre iced tribute to 1950s elegance to trend-led tiers of colour-pop flowers that are almost edible haute couture. The London-based expert cake-makers can adapt recipes to cater to any dietary requirements; which when combined with their focus on making a client's dream cake has made them a must for any seriously stylish wedding.

Bridal Fashion Guide

Browns Bride

Acres of white lace, frothy tulle skirts, spellbinding embellishment and the subject of countless fantasies: the wedding dress. Whether you are a bride who has dreamt of her big day number since she was knee-high, or find yourself flung as a grown woman into the search, the task of finding that one breath taking dress that makes you feel not only like a bride, but is every inch the modern fairytale is a tough one. Fear not.

Home to some of the most sublime wedding dresses in the land from an exclusive cast of talented designers, Browns Bride is our go-to for dresses that are at once heart-racingly beautiful, luxurious and not at all scrimping on romance, yet firmly of a fashion sensibility. Browns Bride is quite literally wedding dress heaven: only the most stylish gowns make it onto the rails of their showrooms nestled on Hinde Street and a dedicated Vera Wang boutique on Brook Street, just across from Claridges. Curated with the same Midas touch as the Burstein family's legendary South Molton Street high fashion boutiques, the knack for finding showstoppers and fledgling stars such as Alexander McQueen - who was discovered by founder Joan Burstein and whose fashion house went on to deliver one of the wedding gowns of the century – translates to an array of wedding dresses that are each and every one a masterpiece. The unrivalled collection boasts Monique Lhuillier, Peter Langner, Mira Zwillinger, Marchesa, Alberta Ferretti, Akira Isogawa, Carolina Herrera, Colette Dinnigan, Delphine Manivet, Elizabeth Fillmore, Reem Acra, Sophia Kokosalaki, Rebecca Street, Valentino, Vera Wang and an oh-so-pretty selection of finishing touches from sashes to tiaras, veils and shoes to add interest and make a look utterly your own.

It's the service though, as individual as it is all about good old-fashioned customer care from its delightfully warm team that makes Browns Bride the store to cross high waters for. Then there's their uncanny talent for plucking your perfect dress with their intuitive grasp of style, fit and personality. Be ready to fall in love, lots.

Which Bride Are You?

Are you Monique Lhuillier's regal romantic? Mira Zwillinger's dreamer? Delphine Manivet's chic Parisian? Every gown here is the dress of a lifetime, and time will be thoughtfully spent guiding you through options to find a gown that fits you, your personal style and wedding aesthetic in addition to being appropriate to your chosen venue and wedding location. A dress consultation starts with a brief look at the particulars of your wedding, how long until the big day (as some gowns may take many months to create) your hoped for look and a glass of Champagne. Take a few images as reference, and bear your style icons in mind when looking at yourself in dresses. But, be prepared to fall in love with the wildcard!

Insider Tips

1. Wear your best blush lingerie, including a strapless bra so that you can see gowns free from the distraction of straps and visible knicker lines.

2. Mimic how you think you'd like to look on your wedding day so that you can get that all important real picture: freshly waxed limbs, simple make-up and your hair worn loose so that you can scoop it up off your face if the dress needs it.

3. Take just your mum, closest friend or wedding planner for company and advice – no more as your head will be in a spin, and you're bound to get conflicting opinions.

4. Move around in your gown to check it has room for manoeuvre (especially important if you like to dance or are required to kneel in a church ceremony).

5. If in doubt, choose the timeless dress rather than the outré one, and style it up with directional accessories such as colour-pop shoes, fresh flower adornments and layers of jewels.

6. At Browns Bride a £25 weekday and £30 Saturday consultancy charge applies, which is fully redeemable upon purchase. You do not need to make an appointment however to view shoes, veils or accessories.

DRESS STYLE GUIDE

Fishtail or Trumpet

Seriously glamorous, the fishtail or trumpet dress hugs the figure before kicking out anywhere from below the hip to the knee. This style looks breathtaking on slim types, creating curves but equally sensational on hourglass and pear shapes as the volume at the hem balances the figure.

Bias Cut

Put simply, this seemingly convoluted dressmakers term simply means the fabric is cut on the bias (or vertically across the weave) so that it sculpts, drapes and shimmies over the body. By turns beautiful on both willowy girls and curvier figures.

Sheath

Modern and understated, the sheath dress flows over the figure for easy elegance that hints at the figure underneath and often features an empire line waist. Looks striking in silk gazar and jerseys, but also does a nice line in lace.

Princess

The eponymous fairytale gown, the princess dress usually features a boned or structured bodice which meets a natural, cinched-in waist line before bursting into a full skirt.

A-Line

Defined by the skirt's shape which imitates that of a triangle; flaring out from the waist in a soft diagonal line. The A-line dress is universally flattering as it skims over the derriere and hips, and shines brightest in heavier fabrics such as damask silk or layered lace which lends a regal quality.

Column

Graceful and chic in that inimitable Audrey Hepburn way, the column gown is quite literally a straight silhouette made for boyish, elfin figures. Add interest by opting for lavish fabrics and embellishment on the bodice.

Tea-Lentgh

Fun, flirty and fabulously fashion-forward, the tea length dress takes its cue from Dior's 'New Look' of 1947, sitting between the knee and ankle. Think Bardot and pair with statement heels.

Ballgown

Playing with drama and volume, the ballgown is a wedding dress classic with a defined bodice (which can be soft or corseted) and sculpted skirt that cries out to be danced in.

Vera Wang

The Story

Fairy tales invented it, Grace Kelly epitomised its beauty but Vera Wang incontrovertibly changed the face of the wedding dress with her endlessly romantic, sensuous and refreshingly youthful creations. A native New Yorker, (which explains the alluring and nonchalant style without a hint of the frou-frou or meringue) Vera was the youngest ever fashion editor of American Vogue at just 23 years old. This is testament to her innate understanding of what the modern bride wants from her 'dress of a lifetime'. A 16-year stint at the helm of Vogue was followed by directing design for Ralph Lauren. Since 1990 however, she has been crafting incandescently beautiful wedding dresses that are distinctive and sculptural. Worn by celebrity brides from Victoria Beckham to Ivanka Trump and Kate Beckinsale, it's impossible not to love Vera Wang for bringing fashion fantasy to the wedding world.

Highlights

Oh Vera, you had us at 'hello' with your striking silhouettes. No one does a mermaid dress, train or origami-inspired drapery quite like this. When textures, whisper-fine corsetry and refreshing colour palettes of lavender, peach (and even smoky black) come together in one of these wedding dresses, it makes for a 3D appeal that any bride would revel in. Vera Wang gowns are known to make you swoon from every angle – even the guests at the very back of your venue will be spellbound by the intricate detail. Flower references play out in exquisite plissé folds that resemble Chrysanthemum blooms and scalloped petals adorn the skirts and trains of slinkier strapless numbers whilst bursts of blizzard beadwork shimmer like dew.

The Dresses

Femininity suffuses every creation – be it the dreamy, 'whipped cloud' tissue organza flange skirts of Diane with its sweetheart tulle draped bodice, or the hand-painted silk Farrah skirt with its soft metallic sheen. As with all the best designers, the collections are continuously improving. Think peplums held proud from the body like 17th century court gowns, Chantilly lace appliqué swathed in fine tulle overlays, asymmetric numbers in stretch Mikado silk with micro pleated bodices, full-on ballgowns with millefeuille skirts. Every dress is available in ivory or traditional white, but why not make a real statement in shades of fondant – they're surprisingly flattering and easy to pull off. Moreover, Vera Wang wedding dresses are as light as a feather, need little accessorising and, when ordered via Browns Bride, fit like a glove.

Dream Bride

If you're looking to light up the room and you love the limelight – these are the wedding dresses for you.

"If you're looking to light up the room and adore being the centre of attention these are the wedding dresses for you"

Marchesa

The Story

Launched in 2009 by Chelsea College of Art and Design graduate friends Georgina Chapman and Keren Craig, Marchesa's bridal collection was born of a shared love of the statement wedding dress. It was also a natural extension of their fashion label which has blossomed to become the toast of Hollywood. In fact, were it not for the lack of the bright gem colours that populate their main line, most of the bridal styles could just as easily pass for the gowns so coveted by stylish fans of the brand - namely Sarah Jessica Parker, Miranda Kerr and Diane Kruger. Drawing on her costume designer's understanding of sculptural lines and drapery, Georgina's wow factor dresses mix with Keren's embroidery skills to create wearable gowns of dazzling detail. First and foremost, they set out to make body-conscious gowns that offered a heart-stopping take on the classic wedding dress. Marchesa is bridal wear's answer to glamour; inspired by vintage and Asian fashion the duo create highly original, exquisite and iconic dresses.

carpet showstoppers to create lustrous beaded embellishment on many of the wedding gowns. Using hints of unusual colours that transform their gowns into distinctive and lovely creations; even the 'Southern Belle' feel of some pearl and lace dappled styles appears sophisticated rather than nostalgic in their hands.

Highlights

Those silhouettes: nipped in by a dropped waist that hugs every curve or taking full advantage of a feminine high waist line that makes waists look teeny tiny; Marchesa certainly know how to make a bride feel like a million dollars.
The best bit? They have carried over the intricate lace and embroidery work from their red

The Dresses

All of Georgina Chapman and co-founder
Keren Craig's wedding gowns have something of
the Haute Couture golden-age ballgown. With
sumptuous layers of pleated tulle pouf skirts, vast
trains and lace appliqué work, there is nothing
obvious here. The collection includes classical
bridal gowns that are reinvented with golden
bead ornamentation creeping over the bodice
(swoon-worthy), to a full-on flurry of fishtail and a
dress fit for a siren with shoulders capped in silk
rosette flourishes. This last gown also showcases an
unexpected twist that is so typical of a Marchesa
bridal dress – a twirl reveals a backless expanse
covered only by the sheerest voile panel and silver
beadwork flowers. From any angle, the spotlight
will stay firmly on you.

Dream Bride

With her instinctive fashion style and her love of
the sensational, the Marchesa bride has all of the
romance without any of the sugary traditionalism.
No meringues or bows, here! Think Nicole Ritchie,
Molly Sims (both Marchesa brides) or the Olsen
twins and pair with crimson shoes.

Rebecca Street

The story

Welcome to the dawn of a new wedding dress era, thanks to the divine designs of Rebecca Street for Browns Bride. Renowned for blending style and substance, Rebecca's beautiful, fluid gowns are the result of skills acquired through her roles as in-house creative pattern cutter with Alexander McQueen, Mulberry, Giles Deacon and through her mainline fashion collections. In Rebecca's hands, (she is also a spiritual healer) silks and deliciously light fabrics are fashioned into wedding dresses that champion femininity. You can quite literally feel the love.

This is how to do wedding dresses without fuss or formality, but with a generous dose of grown-up romance.

Highlights

Appreciated for their sustainable values, each handmade dress in Jacquard, silk satin, chiffon, devoré and crepe instantly ramps up your fashion factor with a billow of train, a little matching jacket or puff of tucked skirt. Then there's the purity of a fluid white floor-sweeper, the ice-cream shades – we could go on for days. Rebecca's gowns have a timeless yet utterly new feel, with a twist of cool. Accents of overlaid fabric, ribbons of sheer tulle and silk and hidden drapery lend each gown graceful style without ever detracting from the poise created from wearing one of these extraordinary numbers.

The Dresses

All of Rebecca's dresses are a joy to wear, like a perfect spring day. Be it in the fresh 60s style of her gowns designed in collaboration with Browns, or in the sinuous bias-cut bridal gowns fit for a goddess, each gown is artful and has a modern understatement. The collection includes pretty and contemporary knee-length dresses with delicate silk devoré overlay, and the sylph-like Waiting for Godet, a bias-cut washed silk gown with a soft silk halterneck draped corset, reminiscent of a John Singer Sargent muse. It is all the more sensational for its delicate graduated 'godets' - little pin ups that add to the grace and waterfall feel of the skirt and train. Made to order, wedding dresses don't come much easier to wear than these beauties that fit like a dream.

Dream Bride

Full of free spirited romance, Rebecca's beguiling wedding dresses would look a picture on any bride, but make us think of Rosamund Pike's English Rose or perhaps most aptly, the original princess bride, Grace Kelly.

Mira Zwillinger

The Story

Could a wedding gown be any more enchanting than a Mira Zwillinger creation? Since 1991, the Israeli designer has been designing gowns of such captivating beauty that they have become a byword for luxurious, dreamy femininity. Meticulously handmade in her Tel Aviv studio using age-old traditions of appliqué, embroidery and nuanced embellishment, it is sometimes hard to believe her gowns are real with their diaphanous fabrics and flawless silhouettes.

Highlights

Mira's collections are full of exquisite dresses and her recent collaboration with her daughter Lihi has brought a touch of street fashion lightness to these joyful creations. For all their traditional bleached white and hand-dyed fabrics, the sensual textures and radiant beauty of Mira's gowns make for a refreshingly modern take on the fairytale wedding dress. Yet, the more girly brides are catered for with super pretty gowns (Charlotte and Beatrice) featuring hints of blush pink peeking from beneath the lace.

Zwillinger's gowns are all about the hand-worked details: tempering froth with sophisticated shapes and strikingly different textures, hand-pleating, crystal beadwork and a unique touch of modernity. Made exclusively

from the finest French and Milanese silks, tulles and laces; each gown bears the Mira Zwillinger signature that layers different laces with appliquéd corded lace flowers. Such detailing lends each dress a nymph-like quality.

The Dresses

The line-up boasts embroidered 'illusion' bodices that float on the sheerest tulle paired with silk chiffon skirts, bold structured brocade gowns in high-waisted shapes dotted with lace adornments at the hem, and classic, heavy white lace styles with optional dramatic chiffon overskirt. All gowns are made to measure.

Dream Bride

The whimsical romantic with an elegant fashion streak: if you are searching for a gown that combines all of the fantastical beauty of lace with a hit of refined modern cut and playfulness, Mira's are the wedding dresses for you. They possess a couture finesse that few of us could dream of, let alone be lucky enough to wear. Think of a latter day Cinderella or Audrey Hepburn's gamine style re-imagined.

Valentino

The Story

For Italian glamour and pure beauty, wedding fashion doesn't come more luxurious than a Valentino wedding gown. Ever since the 1960s, legendary couturier Valentino Garavani has been renowned for his sublime way with sensational linear silhouettes and opulent yet refined detailing: the frill of a collar, the hidden corsetry of a scarlet red dress so fabulous it earned Garavani his own pantone -Valentino Red - and silk chiffons studded with pearl polka droplet beading.

There's a beguiling focus on the feminine form and on striking runway dresses which lives on here, in the work of Pier Paolo Piccioli and Maria Grazia Chiuri's demi-couture wedding styles. Having taken up the helm following Garavani's retirement, they continue his celebrated lineage with styles that are as richly romantic as they are elegant and fashion-forward.

Highlights

Lace, organdie, silk rosette flowers and crisp ivory tones – for a label that does such jaw-dropping things with red frocks, it is little wonder a Valentino wedding dress is every inch the Haute Couture bridal gown. Pretty decorative details such as organza ruffled necklines and white embroidered blossom layers are created in the atelier staffed by skilled 'petites mains' who labour for countless hours transforming each gown into a masterpiece.

"If you're not comfortable, you don't look chic", Piccioli once said. The signature slender and streamline Valentino form, with its sensuously soft silks and unique internal boning and sculpting, does indeed look like a work of art, but is eminently wearable – and practically weightless.

The Dresses

From divine silk columns with a cowl neck revealing a dramatic statement bow twist at the back (very *Gentlemen Prefer Blondes*), to cocktail-length dresses whose long sleeves juxtapose with a frivolous neckline and the fairytale gown reinvented with an oh-so-pretty textured skirt, composed of hundreds of silk flowers topped with a delicate blush bodice; Valentino's wedding dresses marry sophistication with simplicity. Think glamorous, never showy.

Dream Bride

Manna from heaven for any runway bride, Jackie Onassis married in Valentino as did Anne Hathaway. A must for any fan of luminous high-society beauty, these wedding gowns will often move guests to tears, they are so achingly beautiful.

Browns Bride Accessories

You've found your dream dress, now to focus on those finishing touches with the beautiful array of accoutrements at Browns Bride.

A collection of designers that span the gamut from the sparkling (Andrew Prince's crystal jewellery and tiaras, every bit as scintillating as the real diamond thing) to the coquettish with Frou Frou Chic's pretty garters, you can style up your gown as much or as little as you wish. Pearls nod to that something old and Coleman Douglas are the fashion-appropriate

version, whilst you simply cannot go wrong with a red-soled pair of Louboutins. Then there are couture headpieces from Louis Mariette, snuggly yet chic shrugs from Cassin, heirloom-worthy namesake tiaras from Paris Tiaras or opulent pieces from St Erasmus and vintage dress-jewellery from Susan Caplan with her glittering collection of Christian Dior, legendary costume jeweller Weiss Trifari and Givenchy jewels. Just try to remember the words of Coco Chanel when making your choice: "Simplicity is the keynote of all true elegance".

Veil Guide

From the statement veil that adds a little fashion to your gown, to the lacy nuances of an alençon-trimmed number, here's veils decoded.

Fingertip

A veil that reaches just below the waist of your dress, these are available in single or double tiers with a variety of edges from lace to ribbon.

Mantilla

Featuring scalloped edging (often with embroidery, appliqué or lace) a mantilla veil takes inspiration from its Spanish roots and is pinned to the crown of the head with the edge framing the face.

Birdcage

Covering just the head in fine tulle net, this is the ultimate veil for a little retro glamour. Often worn on a headband or hat adorned with embellishment.

Cathedral

A Cathedral length veil sweeps dramatically behind a dress with 140 inches the standard length. Available in edgeless and trimmed styles with one or two tiers, cathedral veils also work with sheath dresses, adding drama.

Chapel

More modest than its big sister cathedral veil, chapel veils are usually 120 inches long but are just as striking.

Juliet Cap

A long-length veil cinched either side of the head and usually adorned with floral or lace detailing at the temples, the Juliet cap veil nods to vintage style.

Bubble

Quite literally a puff of veil folded into a rounded or bow shape (some feature trailing lengths reaching down the back) the bubble is a runway-to-aisle style must-have for the fashion bride.

Beauty

Bridal Beauty Masterclass

1. Let it shine: use illuminating
bases and sweep highlighters across cheekbones
and temples for that inimitable bridal radiance.

2. It's all about every day you, but better. Think
natural, polished skin, sparkling eyes framed with
just the right amount of smudgy defining Kohl
liner, a sweep of sculpting bronzer, a pop of blush
and lashings of waterproof mascara.

3. Use your assets: if you have doe-eyes or are
owner of a plump set of lips, play them up with
accent tones of burnished metallic and muted
berry stains respectively.

4. Raise your eyebrows' game by infilling with
soft brow powder 'pushed' into sparse areas to
create a lush, full look. This will really help frame
your face – and always pluck a day or two before
the wedding to allow the area to calm down.

5. Creating a creamy, radiant complexion is all
a matter of investment: up your intake of fresh
fruit, nuts and Omega 3 rich food for three weeks
before the wedding to see a lit-from within glow
and spot-free skin. And always drink a litre of
water a day – it really does work miracles.

6. Don't fear colour: if your dress is quite simple
or equally heavily embellished, you can contrast
or carry on the aesthetic with striking poppy
coloured lips or twinkling eye shadow. The
golden rule is never both at once.

Featured over the next few pages are a clutch of
some of our favourite make-up artistry talents...

Boe Wright

Bridal make-up and hair should bring out your inner starlet and enhance your best attributes. However, it's mostly to do with letting your natural beauty shine through. A godsend of a make-up artist who trained at the London College of Fashion with a decade of fashion experience under her belt, Boe Wright is a master of the 'less is more' look so many brides aspire to on their big day. With a fashion sensibility inspired by her work with the likes of Vivienne Westwood and the Roxy Music girls, Boe uses the latest products to achieve that perfectly understated, luminous look that still packs a punch. Specialising in make-up and hair for Asian and Afro-Caribbean skins, Boe is an expert in photographic make-up and additionally hosts lessons for hen-parties and brides. But mostly we love her for the way she tailors your make-up so that it is utterly your own, tweaking foundation consistencies and shading, to give you a finish that is you - with flawless genes and skincare habits.

Insider Tip

"Mix a little serum with your foundation for that velvety, second-skin look".

Jo
Adams

What could be more of a treat than being transformed into supermodel material in the comfort of your own home? A favourite with A-listers, runway models, and our very own Quintessentially team, Jo Adams is full of backstage tricks gleaned from London Fashion Week and Jemma Kidd's make-up school. With a talent for lustrous, feminine make-up artistry Jo is incredibly versatile, turning her hand to any look from soft finish radiance to sculpted contours using premium products from the likes of MAC, Bobbi Brown, Chanel and Laura Mercier. Jo can inject style into your big day with as much or as little high-octane glamour as you like to your look, thanks to her knack for glossy hair and false eyelashes. Taking inspiration from the red carpet, Jo is also fabulously talented at hair, creating a camera-ready 'do' to suit you. A lovely, witty and warm pro, she is one of the secrets we would love to keep to ourselves; but given her ability to turn a bride into a blushing beauty and her calming presence on the big day, it would be mean to...

Eyelush

Transforming the flimsiest of

eyelashes, Eyelush are our go-to for extraordinary eyes. Semi-permanent extensions add tear-proof volume for Bridget Bardot style or open up the eyes for that fresh-faced ingénue look when paired with simple make-up. Super long-lasting, the team at Eyelush use pioneering Xtreme lash techniques (which will not harm your existing lashes) at their Kew and Mayfair salons, or even in the comfort of your own home. In fact the whole process is so soothing, it is dubbed 'Beauty Sleep' as so many brides fall asleep and awake to lashes that range from a simple boost to sumptuous sets. Application typically takes two hours, following a thorough consultation.

Karen Beadle

Karen Beadle boasts not only

years of professional experience beautifying the stars, but a real talent for personalising looks. Bridal make-up, after all, is a demanding art: it needs to stay put through tears and flashbulbs - yet look totally like 'you'. Luckily, Karen's way with brushes that sculpt, enhance and highlight combined with a masterful understanding of skin types ensures that this is a given; and that fabled 'bridal glow' doesn't go amiss either. A consultation prior to the wedding includes a make-up lesson, with individualised product, cleansing routine and skincare recommendations to get your big day beauty routine kick-started, too.

QMS Medicosmetics

Any beauty expert worth their salt will tell you that big day beauty and great skin is all in the preparation: regular facials, nourishing moisturisers, restorative massages and bundles of soothing care from within. QMS Medicosmetics is one of our favourite destinations for state-of-the-art skincare technology and miraculous spa therapies.

Nestled in the heart of London, their flagship salon perpetuates the legacy of founder Dr. Erick Schulte. Based on a dermatological philosophy of scientific innovation and naturally powerful ingredients that cleanse, rejuvenate and brighten, the result is skin that appears lit from the inside. The serene spa's spacious treatment rooms offer everything from facials to intensive collagen-boosting regenerative treatments and blemish-busting, corrective pampering. Created with the stressed-out bride-to-be in mind, a specially adapted collection of treatments are complemented by a bespoke range of remedies and products to prolong the effects back at home. Star essentials include the Intravital Supplement for inner beauty, the Alpine Rose-infused serums and Cellular Marine Moisturiser, containing the wonder ingredient Sea Fennel for softly radiant skin. A complimentary consultation identifies what your skin needs in order to be at its 'wedding day best' with a personalised blend of products to guarantee a clear and smooth complexion that is as healthy (no skin-irritating cortisone here) as it is pure and glowing.

MACS Salon

Where to go for the glossiest
bridal hair and make-up? In the heart of Primrose
Hill on the aptly named Princess Road is MACS
salon, a secret bridal beauty destination we were
reluctant to part with...

An award-winning retreat with a 'total'
philosophy that aims to make you look every inch
the iconic blushing bride on the outside, thereby
making you feel utterly beautiful on the inside,
too. There are no empty promises here; the caring
and talented team are as serious about good hair
as they are about making your dreams come true.
This is the time for self-indulgence after all: with
transformative treatments, restorative pampering
and guilt-free "me" time as a bride. The minute you
step inside the stylish and serene space (designed
for VIPs and a starry clientele) you will forget all
the stress of wedding arrangements. It's not just the
fridge full of Champagne or the soothing hands of
technicians that will make you feel this way – it is
the results that speak volumes.

Brides start with a personal style consultation
with a dedicated stylist guiding them through
their look. MACS possess exceptional skill for
interpretation; always keeping things sophisticated,
never fussy. Packages range from luxurious face
and body treatments to skincare consultations, lash
extensions (wave goodbye to mascara-streaked
tears) and make-up inspired by the catwalks yet

always focused on radiance and timelessness.
Ensure you take along a notebook to jot down the
insider tips and personalised guidance you will no
doubt be treated to.

They are, of course, seasoned pros when it comes
to hair at MACS. Besides the suggestions and trials
of arrangements to suit your wedding dress and
individual style, there are several conditioning,
nourishing treatments to get your locks in tip-top

condition. Healthy, luminous and bouncy hair is vital especially if you are to wearing it loose so nurture your hair with regular visits combined with last minute tinctures. The latest addition to their services is a partnership with Great Lengths Hair Extensions for luscious tresses should you wish to go long for your big day: they are surprisingly comfortable to wear, adding volume where needed. In addition, MACS offer a styling service to help wedding guests find their perfect outfit for the wedding, ensuring everyone looks equally glamorous. The whole salon can even be exclusively hired for your bridal party for hours of communal relaxation and heavenly preparation. Take away recommended home-care products and potions to see you up to your wedding day, and call as often as you like for advice. What's more, you can even opt to repeat the preparation on your big day itself in London, and engage one of their sumptuous chauffeur driven cars to whisk you to your venue.

Get Bridal Beautiful
From Corrina McCann

- Condition and care are compulsory: eat a diet rich in nuts, fish, flaxseed, avocados and Vitamins A, C and E for shiny locks.
- The same applies to hair as it does to make-up when it comes to photographs: you always need a little more than you would for every day. Add volume by massaging in a volumising lotion and blow-dry height into the top, using a natural bristle barrel brush.
- Use extensions for extra 'oomph' and rollers for tumbling waves.
- When choosing your make-up and hairstyle, take along images of your style inspirations.
- Keep your face open and hair sprayed back to show off your radiant skin and blush.
- Finish with hero products such as Elnett hair spray, daily cleansing with Dermalogica Daily Microfoliant and good old beauty sleep after some Pukka 'Love' chamomile tea.

Trousseau

Trousseau

So much more than a tradition,

what's not to love about a bride's trousseau brimming with lovely, luxurious things with which to start married life?

What started as a "hope chest" full of ball gowns, silken nightwear and a capsule wardrobe of dresses, tailoring, bags, heels and diamonds symbolising a woman's transition to being a wife has been vastly re-written over the years – but still provides a great excuse to splurge. From honeymoon must-haves to flattering lace lingerie, chic luggage and lots of ladylike treats to see you through the wedding celebrations and beyond, here are our glamorous favourites…

Fox & Rose

A beautiful dress calls

for equally perfect underpinnings. Crammed full as it is of luxurious frills, lace and the purest silk sweet nothings, Fox & Rose is home to lingerie that packs a pretty punch. From gorgeously creamy, stretch silk satin bras with lace trims from Stella McCartney to Jenny Packham couture-inspired negligees and sheer silk robes, the online boutique's range of designs focus on British designers with a little Parisian style shot through for good measure. Shop for soft loungewear treats, kaftans and resort worthy swimwear for your honeymoon, too.

Whether you simply want discreet, flattering foundations for your wedding gown (see the supportive range of bustier bras for sweetheart-neckline numbers) or sensual essentials to see you far beyond your wedding day, there is a style to suit you and your gown. Guaranteed to be his favourite bit of the trousseau, try Mimi Holliday and Damaris for racier numbers. But we did not tell you that…

Amelia Powers

Alynchpin of the classic trousseau (and very good news for bag lovers), a timeless and divine handbag from London-based designer Amelia Powers is just the ticket. In sensational textiles and a variety of hues and patterns from blush python skin to shimmering black leather swung from gilt chain handles, or framed clutches tucked in the nook of your arm; these are the bags we would most like to have and to hold for the rest of our lives.

Feminine, unfussy but fabulous, each bag is made to order in a fabric or palette of your choice in Amelia's London workshop using exquisite craftsmanship and original techniques. The bags are lined with soft goatskin and are impeccably structured. They also pay homage to Amelia's obsession with the golden age of Hollywood, and her erstwhile second occupation as a shaman and all-round cosmic girl as every bag possesses something of the supernaturally beautiful.

Jo Malone London

The renowned British fragrance house that brings brides unexpected scents, sumptuous bath and body care and of course, those covetable candles also offers everything you need to make your wedding day the ultimate multisensory heaven. Working with you to create a signature perfume combination for you to wear on your special day, the team of Jo Malone™ fragrance experts can also layer scents for a sensory experience that transforms a wedding venue. Take your pick from a wide selection of notes from exotic Orange Blossom to the velvety warmth of Amber & Lavender, the crystalline Wild Bluebell or the sweetly rounded Red Roses. A unique blend of scents, candle-lined aisle and liberally spritzed room sprays will fill your venue, carrying guests away with its subtle olfactory allure. Head to your local boutique for a tailored Bridal Consultation, a blissful complimentary Hand & Arm Massage and the most evocative finishing touch to your big day.

Bridesmaids

Ghost

A gown from Ghost is not your normal bridesmaid's gown. Not for those girlish frocks, conventional cuts or overly trend-led dresses trimmed with flounces and frills, but Hollywood-worthy fluid numbers as feminine as they are gorgeous. Cue lace-topped floor-length gowns featuring coquettish slits to the lower thigh, and even dresses in ivory silk satin to mimic a certain Pippa Middleton's royal wedding look in a sophisticated style featuring button-back detail.

In addition to a seasonal collection of Occasion dresses in a palette that ranges from muted hues to lustrous jewel colours with asymmetric straps and womanly silhouettes. There are now 'Dye To Order' bias-cut styles in pretty shades, achieved using a shrinkage garment dyeing process which creates luxurious shades that are incredibly easy to wear and the definition of ravishing too.

Maids to Measure

They give you comfort in times of strife, love, laughter and confidence: so make sure your girls feel as treasured as they undoubtedly are with dresses (almost) as gorgeous as yours. Hitherto the preserve of a lucky few, Maids to Measure design demi-couture bridesmaids dresses that fit the bill for women as individual as they are fashionable. Injecting style, allure and updating the staid bridesmaids dress of old - no criminally expensive, time-warp numbers in shiny satins the precise shade of blancmange here! We love the glorious colour-pop and fondant palette of these gowns in their peach, mint, indigo and antique rose pink available in a fabric of your choice. But the real beauty of a Maids to Measure dress? Much as they let the

bride shine, they'll still make your bridesmaids feel deliriously pretty.

Offering two ways to order your gowns, choose from an online design process of uploading vital stats, choosing your colour, fabric and style choice from fun cocktail lengths to more formal black-tie floorsweepers. This is all you need to complete for sisters India and Sinclair Sellars to rustle up your unique dresses. Dreaming up budget friendly designs at their London atelier, their creations are underpinned by years of bridesmaid duty and experience working for Vera Wang, no less. The dresses are flatteringly draped with personalised twists, full of fashion style with asymmetric shoulders and striking cuts.

Alternatively, you could choose to visit their studio for a real collaborative design process over Champagne and delicious cakes, but knowing that the girls take numerous measurements and each dress has fittings and an alteration included in the price, you can breathe easy knowing your bridesmaids dresses will be wearable whether your girls are waifs or buxom, and quite fabulous with it.

Insider Tip

"Consider slightly different shades from a bouquet for a look that's not too matchy-matchy but refreshing and pretty. Think summer meadows of wildflowers, or autumn berries".

Little Eglantine

If you have not heard of

Little Eglantine, oh my you are in for a treat. Chic, luxurious and delightfully fun to wear, what little girl would not want to wear one of French designer Stephanie Staub's pretty bridesmaid dresses? These made-to-order frocks for flower girls and junior bridesmaids feature piles of embroidery, deep sashes and taffetas with a Dauphine-like rustle; the dresses are beautifully made by a team of 'petites mains'. You can echo the shape of your wedding gown, or tie-in with the grown-up maids' colour scheme: waists cinched in colourful bows and trailing ribbons look particularly lovely. From ivory cap-sleeved frocks with Ladurée shade sashes, to rose silk gowns, or even our favourite – a striking, Parisian grey bracelet-sleeved gown with a hot pink sash – there is something for every wedding style.

Little boys will also no doubt love charging around in the sweet separates: plus fours and Peter-Pan collared shirts or for a more preppy look, cotton shorts with cummerbunds to match.

Lila

These bridesmaids' dresses are the stuff of little girls' dreams. Fantasy gowns with a capital 'F', each is lovingly hand-crafted by this family-run team originally hailing from Greece and now based in London. Bringing a fresh, stylish edge to gowns in fine silk taffeta box pleats, polka-dot organza and luxurious French lace underlay, Lila are our go-to for adorable bridesmaid dresses and exquisite headpieces.

Lila captures the essence of chic yet child-friendly style, so take your pick from classic princess-line designs or opt for couture with bespoke numbers. The designs are made-to-order and intricately hand-finished by highly skilled craftspeople, led by Lila (the mother of the group). Having previously worked for the Greek equivalent of Chanel's Metiers des Arts, Lila brings vintage charm to the dresses without so much as a hint of nostalgia. You can choose to embellish your dress as much or as little as you wish and match the mood, theme and colour scheme of your wedding in sugary or bright shades, sashes or even pick out the flowers in your bouquet with hand-crafted flower corsages. It is the little touches that make these dresses so special, and (to quote many a customer) "just too beautiful to resist". Our favourite part? The handcrafted signature headpieces of intricate clay flowers shaped into wreaths with trailing ribbons at the back. Given such attention to detail it is small wonder that they often go on to become family heirlooms, handed down to flower girls through the generations or worn with Lila's equally lovely christening gowns.

Grooms

Sartorial Groom Style

The secret to cutting a dash up the aisle? There isn't one; but many. What was hitherto the domain of top hats and tails has moved far from the dictated styles of our forefathers. Groom's wear now echoes that of everyday men's fashion - with options to suit (if you'll forgive the pun) every sartorial sensibility. Here, we present our ten essentials of aisle style…

1. Discuss the feel of your big day with your bride to define the style aesthetic – be it relaxed glamour or vintage-inspired elegance – and look for suits that channel this. Be aware that what you choose establishes the dress code for your groomsmen, too.

2. Decide whether you wish to invest in a special, bespoke suit, an off-the peg suit (tailored to fit), or to hire. The bonus is that you can justifiably spend a sizeable sum as you will have ample opportunity to wear your attire again.

3. Choose smart, snappy cuts but err on the side of conservative for a timeless look. Inject a little élan with colour and interesting textures on bow ties, cravats, pocket squares, luxurious shirts and raffish waistcoats.

4. If bold style is your thing, however, don't deviate from it on your big day. Try unusual fabric finishes, shades and contrasting layers: we love inky suits in burgundy and smoke or pale lounge suits (regular suits with notched lapels) in shades of pale tan and grey.

5. If in doubt, pay homage to Bond with a Dinner Jacket or Tuxedo. Remember that you take on the attributes of a suit when you wear it, so a sharply-cut tux will always make you feel dashing.

6. Work with your assets – if you have broad shoulders or beautiful hands, show them off with a slim-fitting jacket or wrist detail and eye-catching cufflinks respectively.

7. There is a reason Savile Row is known as the 'Golden Mile of Tailoring'. It is home to quite simply the best tailors and scissor-wielding sartorialists in the world.

8. Unlike the bride, your shoes will most definitely be seen. Don't disappoint your guests and opt for distinctive styles – try the classics from John Lobb to Church's, but do look to younger brands such as Jimmy Choo. Just be sure to wear them in for all those hours of dancing.

9. Stage a dress rehearsal and try your entire outfit on to check fit, movement, anything amiss and take note of how easily your suit creases.

10. If you're going to sport a tifter, it can only be one from Lock & Co, Britain's finest milliners.

BOW TIE GUIDE

Add a stylish twist – quite literally – to your suit
with our easy-as-pie guide to tying a bow tie…

*1. Lay your collar around your neck, pulling the left
side to 5cm lower than the right.*
*2. Take the shorter right end and cross under the left
end, holding in place with a finger so that you retain
the tightness you want.*
*3. Pass the long end under the short and pull through
in an upwards motion.*
*4. Form the bow by folding around the shorter end
that is dangling down so that it covers the collar join.*
*5. Keep the 'bow' in place with one finger, and drop
the other strand over.*
*6. Pass the loose strand up behind the front loop
pushing it through to form a secure knot. Tug it to
ensure it's fast, then tweak to balance the shape.*

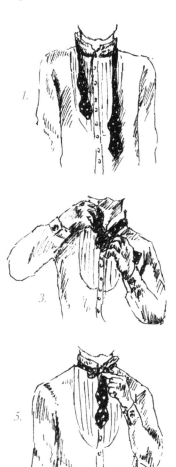

1.

2.

3.

4.

5.

6.

Alexander McQueen

Behind the late designer's
astonishing clothes was one constant: an enduring
love of fine tailoring. Having earned his stripes on
Savile Row and laced this training with his own
genius - as you would expect - a suit from Alexander
McQueen was never just a suit, but a wearable
work of art. With a range of classics each possessing
a distinctive twist, Creative Director Sarah Burton
continues Lee's pioneering legacy with tailoring
far from run of the mill. Perfect for a wedding day
statement, wearing one of these beautiful suits is a
short-cut to impeccable groom style.

Inspired by a romantic heritage of dandies and
Victorian gentlemen, the collection of ready to wear
suits with artful, sharp cuts spans deep cobalt two-
piece wool suits to velvet tuxedos with sweeping
notched lapels. Add some of the accessories
emblazoned with those signature motifs of tiny skulls
and outstretched wings, a piquet bib-fronted dress
shirt and either some black buckled Monk shoes or
feather engraved polished Chelsea shoes; because
as with all things Alexander McQueen, the beauty is
in the details. Newly opened just around the corner
from his training ground at Anderson & Sheppard,
the dedicated menswear boutique is every bit as
captivating as the suits contained within, and will
soon branch out into bespoke tailoring with an atelier
beneath.

Buckleigh of London

Tucked away in a hushed corner of Chelsea, you'll find this celebrated tailor of some of the finest suits and traditional formal-wear for hire in Britain. A champion of the traditional romantic groom's attire so evocative of the likes of Beau Brummell and dashing gentlemen from period dramas, Buckleigh of London's genius suits are as impeccably crafted as they are beautiful. Housing an extensive collection of formal suits to hire from morning suits to dinner suits, evening tails and ravishing accessories to match, there are also miniature versions available in which to dress younger chaps among the wedding party. Think rich black tailcoats, shawl-collared waistcoats and Oxford Brogues, cravats and white silk scarves for that Frank Sinatra look.

The piece de resistance though, has to be their bespoke suits. Specialising in the quintessential tweeds, wools, linens and styles passed down through the generations of this family-run team, grooms can take their pick from dinner suits with double and single breasted detail to opulent midnight-blue smoking jackets in softest velvet and morning suits as unique as you like.

Insider Tip

"Did you know that the term 'bespoke' originates in Savile Row-speak for cloth that was reserved for special clientele, thus to "be spoken for". Even just adding one bespoke touch to your outfit such as a waistcoat or bow-tie can make it feel extra-special".

Good Grooming

Make your bride a happy one
with our expert guide and tips.

1. Don't pull 'that' face when she starts waxing lyrical about napkins and is flabbergasted by your lack of interest in all things frilly and detail-orientated: she will go back to normal post-wedding (we promise) and it's best to just smile and be compassionate.

2. Show interest and take responsibility with the areas of wedmin you feel most comfy with. If you love music, fast cars or have a particularly fervent interest in wine, say so and nominate yourself to look after these duties (and simultaneously dodge being landed with just budgeting and organising hotels – the boring aspects of the groom's involvement). It's all about kick-starting the team work you'll carry on in marriage, and not just about showing up at the church on time.

3. Traditionally grooms cover the cost of the rings, accommodation for the wedding night for the wedding party, the groomsmen's suits and gifts, gifts for the bridesmaids, the honeymoon and ceremony fee. As wedding budgets are so often pooled, this has all but become obsolete, but it's a nice touch to offer to pay entirely for one aspect of the wedding.

4. Don't look back when the celebrant or officient announces the bride's arrival – it's considered bad luck.

5. When she arrives at the end of the aisle beside you, whisper something complimentary about her dress or beauty. We love Prince William's simple but expressive 'Wow!'

6. When writing your speech, you need to thank the bride's mum and dad and the guests for being there; praise the bridesmaids and also your new wife. Keep it what we like to call 'family friendly', and persuade your best man to do likewise. No jokes about past girlfriends, her looks or your new mother-in-law.

7. Sometimes a little vanity is a good thing. Yes, you don't have to go through the palaver of facials, make-up and mani-pedis, but it's a good idea to get your hair trimmed a week before the big day and have your facial hair groomed, too. Digital photography is a lot less forgiving than the eyes of the beholder.

8. Make like the poets of old and write her a little ditty or love letter to enclose with her gift to give to her on the big day. This is when you can be truly soppy and no-one will know the particulars. Plus, she'll love you all the more for it.

9. When it comes to your alcohol intake on the day, think 'merry' as opposed to blind drunk – feast at your wedding breakfast and equally, go easy on the rehearsal dinner liquor.

10. Keep calm and marry on. The Groom's nerves are often maligned, but just remember everyone's there to see you get married because they love you. It's your one day to make like a rock star and have everyone at your beck and call, telling you how awesome you are, so relax and enjoy it as much as you can.

Your On the Day Kit

Should include breath-mints, handkerchief (for mopping brows and dabbing any spills), hand cream to help ease the ring on as you'll find your fingers swell with nerves, a small vial of aftershave from any major fragrance counter and some lip balm or Vaseline for that all important kiss.

Photography

Lucy Tanner

Disarmingly witty, kind, a
'people lover'…There are many reasons to love
Lucy Tanner but we adore her most for her elegant
wedding photography. Established as one of the
top 'snappers' in the land, London based Lucy's
intelligent and stylish work has appeared in some
of the top wedding publications, including Condé
Nast Brides, You & Your Wedding and British Vogue
no less.

A little like having a best friend as your wedding
photographer, she slips straight in to the day with
her warm and discreet manner, winning over even
the most camera-shy of guests. Capturing natural,
intimate pictures of your loved ones and every little

detail, her reportage style creates a moving record
of your day. From those quiet, reflective moments
during morning preparations right through to the
wedding party, Lucy uses her emotional intelligence
to create images that literally show the love and draw
the best from people. Always using natural light to
its best advantage, classic shots in crisp black and
white are at once timeless and fresh, while full colour
images sparkle with life and happiness.

Lucy's way with smiles is not to be underestimated.
Stating that everyone looks beautiful when they are
relaxed and happy, it is clear to see why practically
all her photos feature natural, beaming smiles.
"Nerves can get the better of many brides on the
day so over the years I have developed a little way
of getting people to smile and laugh naturally, as
genuine laughter makes for the most gorgeous shots.
I can't give the secret away but it works wonders and
often has the bride and groom in stitches… Then I
just snap away and capture lovely shots of the couple
at their happiest, most relaxed and most beautiful"

Although flying around the world to shoot
weddings, Lucy is just as happy with simple, pretty
English country nuptials and purposefully tries to
keep her pricing reasonable to reflect this.
She can provide a disc-only package for couples with
smaller budgets, as well as handcrafted boxes full of
prints and bespoke albums for larger spends.

Sarah Critchlow

A **Sussex-based photographer** who clearly has a winning way with cameras and people, Sarah Critchlow takes wonderfully stylish and contemporary wedding photos. Capturing all of those key moments in a reportage style, the easy elegance of her portraits and scene-shots really lets your personality shine through. She invests lots of time in getting to know you, so you can relax and trust she'll capture the wedding pictures you dream of. Looking back on your beautiful album, story book or even just your favourite prints will evoke fond memories of every step of your wedding, from the fun and morning preparations of make-up, to the last crackle-and-pop of the fireworks. Sarah is vastly creative as well as a real professional, working with some of the finest venues in the south (although happy to travel nationwide) she knows how to get the very best from a venue and is a member of the Master Photographer Association and British Institution of Professional Photographers. From Beatles-style shots of the groomsmen striding across a pelican crossing to stolen kisses, her photos do all the talking.

Pippa Mackenzie

What could be better than one extremely talented, award winning photographer with a rare knack for storytelling snapping your wedding? Answer: two of them!

Pippa Mackenzie and Ian Hearnshaw are a husband and wife team that fell in love with the notion of capturing weddings while planning their own nuptials back in 2005. They combine their rich individual experiences in the world of film, graphic design, documentary and fine art photography. The resulting photos speak for themselves - polished images with an almost cinematic quality. Whether in staged group shots or spontaneous reportage stills, every picture is imbued with warmth, vitality and above all - love.

After your initial meeting (we also love them for bringing scrumptious chocolate cake along), Pippa and Ian like to indulge you in an engagement shoot or 'eShoot' to create a bond which allows you to get used to being the focus of the camera's attentions. It's a lovely touch, and means that in addition to their calming and caring influence on your big day, you'll be relaxed and guaranteed a record of your day that is filled with tangible feeling. They offer their undivided time and attention so as to track the story of your day from the hubbub of the morning to the nervous grin of the groom at the end of the aisle, right through to all of the dance floor action. This is another bonus of having two photographers - they can be in two places at once and never miss a trick.

What truly sets them apart, however, is the gorgeous family of books, albums and keepsakes your photos will be turned into. Chiefly designed by Ian who brings his graphic design skills to the fore, their collection of books and albums - Life, Gaia, Passion and Companion - are produced by some of the best manufacturers in the business. There are photo frames and handbag-sized albums too, and in keeping with the Pippa Mackenzie Photography ethos, the 100% recycled paper Gaia book is as green as they come.

Insider Tip

"The key to great wedding photographs is simple: just let go! We like to grab couples for 20 minutes and take them somewhere private—it's often only then that the reality that they are really married sinks in and we get the best shots, which are those full of emotional clarity."

Aneta Mak

Forever. Such a simple word
with its allusions to true love and to things that
never lose their shine and magic, and that you
cherish forever. When it comes to your big day,
those crisp memories may inevitably fade a little,
but luminously beautiful photographs will not. Step
in Aneta Mak, a one-woman photographic wonder,
(and a lovely one to boot) who produces precisely
what we're talking about.

Seemingly everywhere (judging by the resulting
candid shots and caught glances) and nowhere
at once, she melts into the background and takes
some of the most heart-stopping shots of weddings
that we have ever clapped eyes on. From family
formals and fine art portraits to photojournalistic
reportage captured across medium format film,
digital and even Polaroid - you'll have all of the most
memorable scenes including the subtleties, conveyed
in almost tangible stills. Whoever said no-one would
notice your shoes under your wedding dress had
clearly not heard of Aneta. Her magpie-like love of
all things pretty is matched only by her easy manner
with people. She catches the smallest details and
immortalises your flowers, dress, table settings and
stationery with style and grace in her shots.

During your pre-wedding meeting to plot your
vision of the photos, you can opt for an engagement
or 'love' shoot so as to get to know each other and
to feel super comfortable on the big day. Aneta is

known for her punctuality; she'll be there to catch
unlimited shots from the morning's preparations with
its clouds of hairspray, right through to the clatter of
the tin-cans tied to the bumper as you drive away
for your first night as newlyweds. Once developed,
retouched and honed to perfection you'll receive your
images on a DVD to share with loved ones. We dare
you to resist one of the exquisite, fine leather and
silk-bound albums that you can treasure for the rest of
your (happily married) days.

Allora Visuals

When Fred kisses Holly, finally, at the end of *Breakfast at Tiffany's*… Or when Ryan Gosling cries out "I wrote you every day" to Rachel McAdams in *The Notebook*. Especially when Prince Phillip plants that smacker on Princess Aurora. That lump you get in your throat and those rare goose-bump moments when watching romantic scenes in films are, let's be honest, usually missing from wedding videos. Yet the creative team at Allora Visuals, headed by Joshua and Nicholas, are busy putting that captivating magic back into a moving documents of your day. Put simply, their film-maker's eye allows them to tell stories that capture your big day with beauty, personality and in full cinematic style. They meet you to get under the skin of your love story, after which they slip seamlessly into the motions of your wedding, producing your movie with just the right musical soundtrack to match. Oh, and goose bumps are the natural result, every time.

Entertainment

Wedding Smashers

What's the crucial ingredient
that gets guests of all ages knocking over
tables to get to the dancefloor? It is that touch
of magic that the fantastically friendly and
stylish Wedding Smashers have in spades.

Founders Max and Noah met whilst at school
and began their careers on the London club
scene at the tender age of 16. They were joined
by Lucy after she fortuitously spun one of the
boys favourite records at a party (Everywhere
by Fleetwood Mac) and they have been
overhauling the cheesy, staid wedding disco
stereotype ever since. There are now seven
superstar DJs in their agency ready to 'smash'
any dance party. Playing an eclectic mix of
genres, their playlists span 50s rock n 'roll
to current chart hits, Motown to UK Garage
and pure, unashamed Pop. They have graced
the Sex & the City and The Inbetweeners film
premieres and their DJs hold residencies at
The Ivy, Kensington Roof Gardens, Chinawhite
and The Castle Gibson Venues to name but a
few. Each playlist is fully personalised for your
perfect wedding soundtrack, and is anything but
formulaic. Known for their enthusiastic dance
moves and sharp fashion sense, there is no
music snobbery here so if you love a bit of 90s
cheese, or if you are not even that sure of what
you want, Wedding Smashers will still rock the
house down. Get ready for when they spin the
tune that will have everyone from your grandma
to your hippest friends moving like Jagger, and
make sure the photographer is close at hand!

How to create your smashing playlist

1. Grab a bottle of wine, your fiancé (e) and start looking through your own music collection. Spend an enjoyable evening listening to all those songs that make you feel warm and fuzzy inside or alternatively, make you want to jump up and work it like Beyoncé. Write them down, and bring them to your DJ for honing into a playlist.

2. Playlists should match the stages of the party, with more energetic and euphoric songs saved for the middle to last hours.

3. A good rule of thumb if you are worried about pleasing all tastes and ages is to play family-friendly classics in the first half of the evening (think Rolling Stones, The Beach Boys and early Madonna) and go wild with the more current stuff later on.

4. If you hear a song when you're out that you just have to have on your playlist, Shazam is a great little app for finding out the artist and title of the track.

5. Balance the playlist between what guests want to hear and songs that let your personalities shine through.

6. Create a 'Do Not Play' list of any song that makes you cringe such as the 'Birdie Song', 'Hi Ho Silver Lining', 'Agadoo' or anything by Cliff Richard - but give your DJ creative freedom to read the room and play some guilty pleasures if it makes guests happy. There's nothing wrong with a bit of well-timed fromage.

DJ Philly

From 'old school' guilty pleasures mixed with R n'B, to hip-hop, indie, a little electro, funk and quality house, DJ Philly is on our speed dial when it comes to captivating party music.

Working closely with couples to tailor the soundtrack to their party so that every last guest wants to get up and show off their best dance moves, Philly has a unique ability to connect with guests and 'read' a room (as she frequently done with her residencies at Boujis, Pacha and Fabric). One of the trickiest aspects to music for weddings is finding that holy grail of a song that will have every guest from octogenarian aunts to the youngest child up on the dance floor. Philly's way with tunes has had the likes of Johnny Depp, the Black Eyed Peas, Sienna Miller, Timbaland and even Rosie Huntington-Whitely dancing on a table, meaning that this priceless moment is pretty much guaranteed.

Urban Soul Orchestra

For string ensembles with a unique twist, to DJ sets featuring live string arrangements and big band music to get a party started, enter Urban Soul Orchestra. A versatile collective of world-class musicians who have performed with the likes of Mick Jagger and Take That, they have over 20 years' experience. Offering a complete soundtrack to your big day, from accompaniment up the aisle to chilled-out background music during the drinks reception and dinner. As the evening progresses, they really raise the roof; whether with a golden age of glamour Swing Band or a Big Band performing all of the latest hits, guests are lured onto the dancefloor – where they often remain all night!

Katya Herman

What could be lovelier than the sparkling sound of a harpist drifting through your wedding reception? Katya Herman makes for an enchanting addition to any wedding, creating a romantic atmosphere with her gilded full-size concert harp or smaller electric version. Trained at the prestigious Guildhall School of Music and Drama, she has gone on to play at the Royal Albert Hall, St. James' Palace, Windsor Castle and even Vivienne Westwood fashion shows. With a wide repertoire that ranges from classical to jazz with smooth and sultry Bossa Nova rhythms, strident Flamenco numbers and Celtic love reels to boot, Katya also teams up with a vocalist, cellist or flautist on request.

Sharky & George

Everyone loves children at a wedding, but what to do with the little nippers when they get fed up with the cutting of the cake, speeches and grown-up bits? Simple. Place them in the capable and exuberant hands of Sharky and George's experienced team of entertainers; armed with a novel array of props and good old-fashioned fun that will elicit squeals of happiness from children aged 3 – 12 years.

Whether you prefer to whisk the younger guests away to give your adult guests a chance to let their hair down or to keep the children involved throughout the day the options are many. The fully CRB checked team will organise imaginative activities that have been thoughtfully planned from a child's point of view. From launching Chinese paper lanterns adorned with messages for the happy couple, to treasure hunts and games such as Sharky's Footsteps (grandmother's footsteps with sweeties involved, yum!), everything has been designed for a wide age range so they can all play together. After all, which age group doesn't enjoy tug of war, bubbles or catapulting water-bombs (don't worry - not messy). Babies and toddlers from 0 – 3 years can also be looked after by Sharky and George's nannies who will include the littlest ones as much as possible in the games. Our favourites? Just picture little gaggles of children weaving through the guests offering their home made chocolate truffles as you polish off your pudding. Then watch out for a miniature dance crew with glow bracelets, UV paint, fancy dress and some freshly taught moves unleashed on the dance floor – a literal flash mob! Exhausted after a hard day's fun, the children can flop in front of a DVD until their parents are ready for bed too.

144 ∞ 145

Transport

Arrive in Style

Make your entrance an extraordinary and A-list-worthy one. Life's too short after all to arrive in anything less than something fabulous. Whether you simply need to get from your parents house to the church or civil ceremony venue, or you are looking for a flotilla of vehicles for your wedding party and a getaway car for later, there is a host of elegant options to inject something special into the proceedings. Anything is possible: from the pageantry of a horse and carriage to the romance of a gondola, the glamour of a sports car or even the novelty of arriving by reindeer-drawn sleigh in the snow.

Insider Tips

- Create a thoughtful, relaxed big-day atmosphere by organising transport for guests to and from your wedding venue – especially if you have chosen a rural, hard-to-find location or have separate ceremony and reception venues more than walking distance apart. Even pre-ordering a fleet of taxis to collect guests at the end of the evening is a nice touch and they will really appreciate it.
- Provide treats for guests if the journey between your ceremony and reception venue is anything over 20 minutes, if only to stop reception drinks hitting an empty tummy.
- If you are on a budget, do not be scared of asking guests to chip in with coach or taxi fares.
- Go all-out and ask your chosen hire company to dress your vehicle in ribbons, flowers and perhaps a gorgeous 'Just Married' sticker from notonthehighstreet.com for a finishing flourish.
- Always give yourself leeway with timing, especially with weekend weddings when traffic is usually heavier. Also make time for photos on arrival with your car or carriage.
- Think about how big your dress is when choosing a wedding car and forewarn the company in advance of arranging a viewing so you do not give the game away with a "well, my skirt has lots of layers of tulle so..."
- Ensure your chauffeur has an umbrella on-board for any showers.
- Give your driver's mobile number to your chief bridesmaid or your delegated person in charge, to liaise directly in case of any delays or difficulties.
- Prepare a CD of songs that will get you in the mood and ask your driver to pop it on for the journey.

JD Prestige Cars

Glamorous? Check. Grand?

Check. When it comes to making a dazzling entrance, little beats an elegant wedding car from JD Prestige Cars. Put it down to your groom's inner James Bond if you will, but these are the sort of cars men dream of and will likely ignite envy among every male guest as you glide up to your venue in a flurry of flash bulbs. Dressed in ribbons and polished to a sheen, with the softest leather interiors for a super comfy ride; it is small wonder brides are also frequently as smitten. The fleet ranges from new Rolls Royces to Bentleys, Ferraris to Aston Martin DB9 Supercars for a film-star style arrival that never fails to turn heads. Chauffeurs are dressed in polished livery to soothe any jitters en route and a spin around the block if you arrive before the obligatory 20 minutes late. Why not hire a posse of high-rolling beauties to transport your bridesmaids and parents to the ceremony for a seamless arrival? Or why not book a supercar for your fiancé as a surprise so that no one misses out on any of the big day pageantry.

Insider Tip

"On the big day itself, it is all too easy for the day to pass by in a blur of catching up with loved ones and hardly spend any time with your new spouse. Book in a half-hour slot with your chauffeur to go for a spin, and bask in your newly-wed status. You will be really glad you did".

Great Escape Classic Car Hire

Purveyor of all things 'va-va-voom',
Great Escape Classic Car Hire boasts a fleet of
over fifty beautiful classic and performance cars
to hire for a terribly stylish arrival on your big day.
Usually hired on a self-drive basis requiring either
the father of the bride or a friend to speed you to
your ceremony, you can opt in some cases for a
chauffeured car and opt for coloured car ribbons
and flowers to tie your chosen car in. From a sky-
blue Aston Martin DB6 (owned and chauffeured
should you so wish by the charming Crispin) to a
cool white Jaguar E-Type convertible, Bentleys and
an Austin Healey 3.9 V8, why not make like Prince
William and take your new bride out for a spin with
the traditional empty cans rattling at the rear…

Finishing Touches

not on the high street. com

As the old adage goes, it is the little things that make the difference: never is this truer than when it comes to this treasure trove of all things original, notonthehighstreet.com. A must-visit for the modern wedding couple, adding just a few touches and embellishments from their easy-to-use (and beautifully designed) online marketplace ensures your big day reflects your personal style.

An inspired choice for thoughtful couples, there is a distinctive selection of bespoke favours and decorations, personalised wedding invitation suites, bridal accoutrements and enough bunting to cover the breadth of Britain with which to complete the picture you had envisaged of your wedding day. Whilst many brides love the idea of making everything themselves by hand with DIY projects, after all, few will find they have the time once the full-scale wedding planning begins. Established in 2006 with just a hundred sellers, today over 3,000 independent creative small businesses lovingly hand-make or source thousands of original products found here. Whether inspired by understated glamour, the quintessentially British country wedding or something utterly unique, a visit to notonthehighstreet.com yields all of the elements you will need to transform a setting from the ordinary to the extraordinary.

Specially curated to offer a broad selection of truly unique and customisable products, nothing here is tacky nor too expensive - just inspired, stylish and romantic. Deservedly our first port of call when we are seeking personal touches to add that extra certain something you cannot put your finger on, you need not be a 'creative' either to achieve the look from all of those moodboards and tear-sheets you have doubtless created by this point. Notonthehighstreet.com makes sure it is as easy to keep up with the latest decoration trends, as it is to stay true to your own individual style and as with all of the best websites and unexpected content, there is its very own inspiring wedding blog, tietheknotonthehighstreet.com to peruse too. Oh, and want the hand-stamped place cards you have seen in blue but would prefer them in damson? All you need do is ask the seller directly, via their product page, or speak to a member of notonthehighstreet.com's helpful customer service team.

Vicky
&
James

I LOVE
YOU

Greathire

For furnishing and finishing touches there's a great selection from the never-ending haul at Greathire to suit every wedding style and environment.

Once you've chosen your venue, it's time to personalise your space with tables, chairs, candelabra, settees, decorative accessories, embellishments and everything in between. We discovered their compelling blend of old favourites mixed with new, fun and relaxed furnishings some while ago, and have made Great Hire our go-to for their seamless, innate style and painstaking attention to detail.

When it comes to transforming your venue, the crack team at Greathire will guide you through their thousands of furniture sets (all equally striking) and clever designs at either their showrooms or through a concise online process to bring your big day vision to life. Known for their distinctive and superlative quality goods, they constantly innovate and refresh their collections, but whatever your choice, the inspired and sophisticated aesthetic that defines all of the furnishings will ensure that they look like they permanently belong with the space. No superimposed or discordant style, here – just plenty of gorgeous items to create the atmosphere to suit you and the setting.

Whether it's a glamorous city affair, a blank canvas marquee wedding in the countryside or even a stately home with oodles of individual and varied spaces to dress, there are chic and comfortable solutions to match every wedding. White Louis XVII dining chairs are crisp and fashion-forward when paired with round white tables and crystal-drop candelabra. Ornately framed mirrors work well with Paul Antonio's calligraphy-inscribed wedding breakfast menus. Or how about an al fresco, LA pool side feel with wicker chairs teamed with Palm Beach wooden sofas, hot pink and chartreuse cushions, hurricane lanterns and palm trees? Colour schemes are made easy with seat cushion pads in every conceivable shade, silver gilt tables and elegant poser tables in anything from jet black to vermillion. Our favourites have to be the velvet ottoman stools that are ideal for creating a louche lounge area, and the folding screens for a dress-up boudoir for your photobooth.

All of the furniture is installed by the professional (and strong!) Greathire in-house team who will work around the clock to set your space up. Better still, they will leave without a trace that they were ever there.

Seating Plans

Grab a bottle of wine, your fiancé and a sheet of A1 paper – it is seating chart time, otherwise known as the wedding day equivalent of a military operation (with a little matchmaking thrown in for good measure).

1. A good rule of thumb is to group guests by interests and to take account of their relationships to each other.

2. If you have any unfailingly witty guests, try and seat one per table. Laughter is the very best ice-breaker.

3. By all means dabble in playing cupid by seating single guests together, but only on the same table (and preferably opposite so they can make eyes at each other) never next to each other as: a) it takes some of the thrill of the chase away and b) it is too flagrant.

4. Adopt a stiff upper lip when it comes to family politics. They really should not air their issues on your big day anyhow, but do be kind: best not to seat any hostile relatives together unless you do not mind a spot of fisticuffs – verbal or otherwise.

5. Do not be afraid to mix up generations but always seat at least two couples per table who know one another so no-one feels adrift.

6. Handle guests without a plus-one or date with care – we have all been there one time or another. Try and seat them on a mixed table of friendly faces.

7. Avoid your seating descending into a social experiment by clustering friendship groups together but throw in a few wildcards who you think will gel.

8. Beware of the dynamics of exes and new partners – seat at least four couples apart.

9. We love including a little card with each guest's place setting that gives a little teaser about the person sat next to them. It can be how you met them, an interesting fact about them or a question such as 'Get Lauren to explain how she came to be on the top of a mountain-side in the Andes with just a goat and a bottle of Absolut Vodka for company'.

House of Hackney

Since discovering this wildly
creative East London designer's furnishings and
glorious fabrics, we have not been able to think
of a better way to dress a room than with a few
carefully selected, statement pieces. Presentation
is everything, after all. Put a different spin on a
photobooth using a bolt of their ombré-effect
Dalston Rose fabric for a backdrop, or serve cream
teas with an array of their deliciously whimsical
cake stands, teapots, cups and saucers for a stylish
touch that is anything but chintzy, and most
definitely cool.

Snow Business

Summery weddings with their
sun dappled lawns flanked by flowery borders
are all very well, but for the most wonderlandish
of settings any time of year, look no further
than these leaders in all things snow. Using
both recycled and biodegradable products, the
specialists in artificial snow and wintry special
effects at Snow Business create such realistic
falling snow and snowscapes at their HQ at the
aptly named The Snow Mill. Any wedding venue
can be transformed for an enchanting, utterly
convincing snowy backdrop. The team can bring
their bag of festive tricks to any location across
the world, and always leave it exactly as they
found it.

Ideas Box

Hire one of Ideas Box's tricycles laden with goodies from ice cream to candy floss, popcorn, fresh doughnuts and crêpes or that great British classic, Pimms, for a novel and delightful addition to any wedding. The cheese or waffle tricyles make for perfect late-night munchies when guests are ravenous after all that dancing. Choose from over 400 cheeses, served from slate plates with a variety of biscuits and chutneys from caramelised onion marmalade, to plum & ginger.

With their retro Pashley trikes and debonair manner, they can add a vintage feel or even provide chic frozen cocktails of Snow Cones laced with spirits and also offer the original chocolate fountain (just beware the white dress!) with tumbling rivers of Belgian Couveture chocolate and fruit nibbles to dunk. Unique flavours are what really set them apart though, with everything given a gourmet twist. The celebrated ice-cream comes in a plethora of flavours make for a welcome shot of cool on a hot summer's wedding day. We love American apple pie, chocolate nut brownie, crushed strawberry and the sorbets of lychee, autumn blackberry and chic twists on alcoholic desserts with delicious Champagne or even mulled wine sorbets. The most fun you can have on three wheels.

The Real Flower Petal Confetti Company

Just picture the scene:

thousands of the prettiest petals sprinkling over you as you make your exit from the ceremony, confetti fluttering down like blossom on your perfect first moments as husband and wife. Or why not arm your flower girls with baskets to walk in front of you up the aisle, scattering flowers as they go? Either way, the delicate loveliness of the confetti from The Real Flower Petal Confetti Company makes a romantic addition to any wedding. Rumour has it they supplied the Royal Wedding with their biodegradable petals from delphinium, rose, hydrangea, bougainvillea, lavender, bluebell and wild flowers. Sold by the pint, each bag allows for 10 good handfuls of the confetti which comes in shades from ivory to baby pink, lilac and fuchsia. Bundled into sweet parchment cones, they also sell leaf skeletons perfect for autumnal weddings, and horseshoes wrapped in ribbon for luck (we love their idea of hanging it around any attendant pooches' necks).

Faust's Potions

Wedding favours needn't mean predictable little sacks of sugared almond dragees or soon-forgotten trinkets. Something of an insider secret (and staple with our team for inclusion in guest wedding welcome packs) for favours that friends and family are sure to thank their lucky stars for, Faust's Potions are little shy of a bottled miracle.

Designed for the night owl and hedonist – into which category wedding guests must surely fall – these little vials of 'potion' composed of all-natural ingredients come as a pair of tinctures to prevent and then ease the effects of partying. A restorative blend of nutritional supplements, vitamins, herbs and a host of secret ingredients with no added sugars or artificial flavourings, the potions - 'Asleep' and 'Awake' - contain honey, milkthistle, vitamins B1, B6, B12, Griffonia seed extract and ginkgo Biloba, Guarana, ginseng, green tea, Vitamin B and complex Vitamin C respectively. Packaged into elegant bottles and then enclosed within a discreet box, they offer a boost and soothing remedy for those inevitable hangovers, jetlag, post-wedding blues and general fatigue – caused by too much dancing, we suspect.

Boothnation

Why not have one of

Boothnation's sparkly numbers in the corner? Surely the most fun you can have at a wedding, a photobooth captures all of your guests in impromptu photos. With a selection of booths that range from glittery traditional styles to shiny silver air-stream caravans (for the retro fabulous version), whichever you choose, guests always make a bee-line for them, posing for the happiest document of your big day. All of the booths are kitted out with professional beauty lighting, a high-quality digital camera, wind machine, and can even be personalised especially for you. Available in a range of packages including unlimited prints, charming staff to man your booth, an online gallery accessible for up to two months after the event, and CDs of all images, Boothnation offer exemplary service, too. A concept created by award-winning portrait photographer Seamus Ryan in a bid to catch people at their most spirited, we love them giving weddings such an injection of wit.

Insider Tip

"Make like Hollywood stars and create a dressing-up boudoir next to your booth equipped with cigarette holders, bow-ties, top hats, jewels and furs for some silver screen action. Or why not get guests to play out your favourite fairy-tale with themed props?"

The State of Grace

Hitherto the preserve of

red-carpet stars and super-models, meet one of London's best kept style secrets for that all-important injection of personalisation to your big-day look, The State of Grace.

Via her glittering one-stop shop, Lucia Silver offers a head-to-toe design and styling service that will make you not only look, but feel like a million dollars. Who would not want a little of that on their wedding day?

Whether you are just at the start of the hunt for your dress, or are seeking a statement piece to make your outfit feel utterly your own, the service offered (by appointment only) at The State of Grace's London showroom makes it a breeze. Lucia's designs and styling having graced shoots with some of the world's most iconic and gorgeous women, from Jerry Hall to Keira Knightley, Paloma Faith and the royals, show how masterful she is at the bespoke alchemical touches. There are dresses straight from the silver screen, jewels both vintage and modern, hand-sequinned and beaded shrugs, capes, veils, shoes, bags, belts, headpieces and so much more to put a unique spin to your wedding day look (and simultaneously nail that something old and new).

There is, after all, so much more to a breath-taking bride than just a frock, but as Carrie Bradshaw would have it, it is all about 'styling it up'.

Philip Treacy

Is a wedding ever complete

without hats? Whether you are a guest, the mother of the bride or the bride looking for something more daring than a tiara, good millinery is the way forward, especially if it is courtesy of the fabulous Philip Treacy OBE - without doubt Britain's greatest hat designer.

Adored by royalty and the fashion firmament including Sarah Jessica Parker, the late Isabella Blow, Alexander McQueen, Givenchy and Chanel, he is nothing short of a fashion legend. Philip also designed no less than 36 hats for the royal weddings of the Duke and Duchess of Cambridge as well as Prince Albert II and Princess Charlene of Monaco. It would be fair to say that he loves a wedding. He first fell in love with fashion (and those hats) peering through the curtains of his childhood home in the tiny Irish village of Ahascragh to the church opposite, watching as the stylish guests arrived for the impending nuptials. "They were the equivalent of fashion shows to me. The dresses that people wore - I could not believe them. It seemed so glamorous to see these creatures appear in these extraordinary clothes, as we did not have much glamour where I come from", explains Philip. He has never looked back from his humble style beginnings; running up costumes for his sister's dolls and gathering feathers from the

family's game birds to work into the plumage of his remarkable tifters.

"I make hats because I love hats. They make you feel good whether you are the observer of the spectacle or the wearer." Cue fun and fantastical styles from indigo pillbox shapes wrapped in turban-like silk with a shot of cerise gauze bursting from the side to chic, simple caps topped with spirals that evoke unicorns. There are hats for every pocket, with staple trilbies and fedoras making an accessible entry point right through to couture creations. Grab yourself one of these toppers to transform your outfit, and you are set.

Insider Tip
From Philip Treacy

"A hat can completely change the personality of the wearer, makes them stand differently and walk differently. People think sometimes that people who wear hats want to show off. But human beings, since the beginning of time, have always wanted to embellish themselves. So hats have been around since the year dot. Wear yours with guts and guile"

Katy Scarlet Taylor

If like us, you have ever lusted after the inimitable style of icon Sarah Jessica Parker with her city chic-meets-fashion-forward cool, or the grace of Audrey Hepburn, look no further than top fashion stylist Katy Scarlet Taylor. When it comes to your big day look and the styling for your whole wedding party, under our resident stylist's guidance, bridal has 'fabulous' written all over it. No millefeuille meringues, starchy gowns, ill-advised fascinators or staid wedding belles here.

Acutely aware of the frustrations many brides feel when trying to find a gown that will suit their style, Katy works very closely with them. Creating personalised mood boards and hunting out the most breathtaking and sophisticated wedding dresses from top London boutiques, advising on hair and make-up from her little white book of secret sources, this is a head-to-toe service. It is full of impartial advice and expert know-how that makes being a knockout bridal beauty as easy as pie. Think of her as your fashion fairy-godmother…

A Contributing Editor on this very book, Katy has worked extensively with nearly every bride we have planned a wedding for, putting a stylish stamp on their bridal look to ensure they face their day with poise and confidence. Never underestimating the power of good heels and accessories, Katy can beautifully transform an outfit and can work on any budget through clever tricks and innovative ideas. Having worked in the fashion departments of Vogue, Grazia, InStyle, Tatler and GQ Style, (she does a mean line in men's styling too) Katy knows an iconic look when she sees it. Deploying skills she usually reserves for celebrities and luxury brands like Gucci, MTV, the ELLE Style Awards and Sotheby's Diamonds, you will emerge a flawless bride; as comfortable in your wedding dress as in your favourite jeans. Complete with Manolo Blahnik heels and shiny mane of hair, of course.

Big Day Survival Guide

Do not panic! Quintessentially Weddings unveils its top tricks and tips on beating the wedding day stresses.

1. Do not be afraid to shake up tradition – you should not feel obligated to have a ritual or item just because 'it is what you do' or to appease parents. Send your bridesmaids down the aisle in front of you if you like, do not throw the bouquet, get everyone up midway through your first dance and stay and party to the end if you want to.

2. Play safe, and ask your groom to carry some emergency cash for any unforeseens such as running out of wine.

3. Breathe! The stress hormone cortisol raises your adrenaline levels, increases the likelihood of mistakes and aggravates your skin so you may end up more of a flushing than a blushing bride.

4. Smile – it has a radiant effect and adds to your bridal allure.

5. Remember Carrie's wise words to Charlotte if and when things go wrong: "the worse the wedding, the better the marriage". It might not be strictly true, but helps to remind you not to worry about the little things.

6. Visit Metcheck.com the week before the wedding and draft in any brollies, blankets or wellies you might need to keep you and your guests warm and dry.

7. Brief one 'Scout Leader' friend (you know the type, always know what the traffic is like ten minutes before the rest of you do, who keeps calm and always has some Alka Seltzer, safety pins and plasters to hand) on your running order for the day. Give them your sheet of contact numbers and place them under strict instructions to not let you know if something goes awry, and to keep the Champagne coming if it does.

8. Stash a pair of comfy shoes at your venue for when those heels start to pinch so you can dance till the sun rises.

9. Do make like many American couples and opt for a 'first look' before you walk up the aisle: meet your groom somewhere private and show each other your wedding finery – it is also a great way to quell nerves.

10. Embrace the day: try to ditch your worries, relax and protect your happy experience of the day by being a gracious host and laughing off any mishaps. That is your only job on the big day: to get married and have fun!

Your on the Day Kit

Mints, blotting paper for those dreaded shiny patches, bobby pins, paracetamol, Party Feet to keep you dancing all night long, lip balm (we love Eve Lom Kiss Mix) for that all important kiss and a little perfume to keep you smelling sweet.

Gift Registry

The Wedding Shop

There are wedding lists, and then there are luxury wedding gift lists. The Wedding Shop's gift registry service falls firmly into the latter category, brimming over with the most undeniably stylish and homely items from 250 brands with which to fill your new marital home.

Established in 1990, The Wedding Shop is a purveyor of tailored home and living wares, revered for its personal service. Beyond the rows of elegant treasures, handmade rarities and the best basics for a life together, everything at their Chelsea, Fulham, Selfridges, or Dublin Brown Thomas emporiums speaks of characteristically good taste that is masterfully matched to your style. A wedding list from The Wedding Shop reads like a one-stop-shop design for life, only a great deal more fabulous. Featuring homely interior furnishings from the likes of Ralph Lauren Home, tableware from the great British craftsmen of Wedgwood to striking Alain Thomas parrot-adorned Haviland ranges, it's all about the covetable edit.

As the leading independent registry service, the consultants have the added boon of being able to pluck the most tempting fixtures and accoutrements from a surprisingly accessible spectrum of price points. From household names to pieces from up-and coming-designers or unique one-off items, there is something at The Wedding Shop to suit all of your guests' budgets. What's more, should they not stock a particular item they can source it direct from the supplier and add it to your list. Think of it as almost a couture experience; adjusting and sending special requests all over the world. The possibilities for putting your stamp on your married home and life here are virtually endless.

Creating a wedding list with The Wedding Shop is a joy, not simply for the fact there is plenty to fall hopelessly in love with. Dedicated consultants get to know you and your back-story, lending the whole experience a uniquely personal feel. This ensures you get maximum use and pleasure from every item in your selection, and equally your guests are safe in the knowledge they are giving you something you'll adore. It's all part of the highly individual attention that they pride themselves on, and for which we have admired them for over 20 years. The Wedding Shop experience essentially comes down to thoughtfully selecting a timeless wedding registry, whilst also providing a service that is as quick as it is stress-free.

You can be confident that a selection curated by The Wedding Shop will mean your new 'married' home will be just as you envisaged. Be it a cosy cocoon filled with plush furnishing, M'Heritage Mauviel copper pans and William Yeoward

glassware, or a light-filled contemporary space boasting bold printed textiles by Missoni Home and Le Creuset cast iron dishes in hues of red, aubergine or turquoise – style is of the essence. A significant advantage to creating your list with The Wedding Shop is the option to alter your original list until some months after the wedding day. This means that should you wish to complete a dinner service or opt-in items that had previously not appeared in your selection, it is easily accommodated by your consultant.

HOW IT WORKS

Following an initial consultation, either in person in one of the glamorous showrooms or remotely over the telephone or internet, an initial wish-list is devised.

You may wish to opt for two consultations to give yourselves time to mull over choices; these consultations are available on weekdays, evenings and weekends by appointment to suit you. Your list is then made available online and in-store, while you will be given piles of lovely gift registry inserts to enclose with your stationery, so that your guests can handpick from the collection. Guests can add personalised notes to you should they wish, and you can publish messages to all guests thanking them or suggesting which items you would plump for from the remaining selection.

Guests are updated (as are you) when gifts have been selected so that everyone can monitor what is available, and you can adjust your list should you change your mind. You can't beat twinkling Baccarat crystal ware, Alexander McQueen coffee table books, or Nigella Lawson cookware.

Once you return from honeymoon, the list of purchased gifts can be reviewed again before making your final order. Two free deliveries are available in London as part of the complimentary service, as are two in the Republic of Ireland for Brown Thomas orders. The majority of orders should find their way to you within eight to ten weeks, and additionally, should you not wish or be ready to take delivery of your items; The Wedding Shop can store them for up to six months. As part

of their service, The Wedding Shop also offer a lifetime 10% discount to couples who register their gift lists with them.

The freedom of choice, with so many delightful things to choose from, mixed with flawless customer care is what marks The Wedding Shop out as our go-to destination for the most stylish beginnings to married life. A gift list to marry for!

not on the high street. com

Get ready to fall in love many times over. Dusting down any staid notions of the wedding gift list, this Wedding Gift List Service is a breath of fresh air boasting a vast array of unique and meaningful must-haves to fill your newly married life.

The allure of a notonthehighstreet.com Wedding Gift List is easy to define: a catch-all of stylish, creative and delightful things for your newly married life, mixed with the closest you will come to good old-fashioned personal service online.

All of the home furnishings, interior accessories and stylish lifestyle products you'll find at their online marketplace are made and sourced by 3,000 of the very best home-grown small businesses, meaning you really won't find the same collection anywhere else. From framed maps documenting where you first met, to hand-carved oak cheese boards etched with your names and wedding date, or chic retro weighing scales, everything is created or sourced with care by craftsmen and independent retailers from across the UK.

Setting up your Gift List is incredibly easy, and can be done in a matter of minutes – it'll be hard to resist registering once you've seen the selection of products on the site. You'll be able to add goods immediately using the list builder, and edit or change as much as you like at any time. Open your wedding list straight away, or hide it from view until you've sent your invitations, and each time you log in to your list you'll be able to see what has been purchased – or, you could choose to keep it all a surprise until the big day.

Elegant notification cards are provided free of charge upon request, to be slipped into invitations, and the whole system is a doddle for you to use and your guests to peruse. Those less web-savvy can place their orders over the phone, and there's even a contribution feature that allows friends and family to chip in towards more expensive items on your list. Once gifts have been purchased, your guests can request delivery to their own address, or have things sent direct to you with a personalised message. Quite simply, there's no Wedding Gift List Service less ordinary.

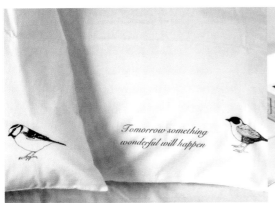

Tomorrow something
wonderful will happen

A & J
THE OLD RECTORY
29TH MAY 2012
CHARLIE'S SUNDAY ROAST

Jonathan & Jenny
New Place, 24th September 2011

Honeymoons & Thereafter

Quintessentially Travel

After all those months of

planning comes the holiday that dreams are made of. Whilst the appeal of days spent lazing by an infinity pool with a cocktail in hand certainly remains undimmed, why not let experts Quintessentially Travel become your passport to an unforgettable, couture honeymoon? With a passion for travel many reserve for their beloved, whether you yearn for a desert island all to yourselves, an adventurous African Safari or indulgent Cambodian spa retreat; they are experts at finding that 'holy grail' destination. Somewhere you'll never forget yet equally never want to leave...

When Booking…

Quintessentially Travel can be on hand from the moment you enquire, until you return, and for everything in between. Make the most of their insider knowledge and top tips to ensure your honeymoon is unique. From recommending tantalising local cuisine, to organising a sunset dinner with your own personal chef, and advising on soothing spa treatments to booking an adrenaline driven activity, they will be there at every step.

Quintessentially Travel's Honeymoon Hotlist

For the key blend of raw beauty, inspiring experiences and picture perfect beaches, we

recommend combining a trip to Sri Lanka with the Maldives - offering the perfect balance between exploration and relaxation.

Alternatively, for those seeking a vibrant and bohemian destination, there is Morocco's kaleidoscope of colour, riads and exciting experiences. Unwind with a hamman massage, head to the hills on horseback, or spend a night under the stars while camping in the desert.

Finally, providing a slower pace and offering true island paradise, we recommend the beautiful North Island of the Seychelles. A stunning bolthole to escape the world, let this heavenly island set the tone for the rest of your life.

Don't Travel Without

You should never depart without vaccinations and visas if travelling to more exotic locales, always pack your camera and our itinerary so that you know all of the extraordinary spots nearby you need to see! Also keep our phone number close at hand as we can offer not only peace of mind and niche insider knowledge, but an on-call concierge service whilst on your travels that can help you maximise your honeymoon adventures, add to bookings and help if (heaven forbid) anything goes wrong.

Daios Cove

Some places just seem to have 'it'. That feeling of paradise here on earth – and Daios Cove Luxury Resort & Villas is certainly a honeymoon hideaway straight from heaven. Nestled in a private bay with pale gold sands, cerulean sea and the sweet scent of lavender and thyme wafting around you on the northernmost tip of Crete, this glamorous resort seemingly rises out of the ruggedly beautiful cliff face.

Channelling relaxed and modern luxury fashioned in ivory stone and sheer glass architecture with plenty of comforts, it is easy to see why you might be tempted never to venture further than your own private pool villa. With the Cove Club, a full concierge service, complimentary wedding and honeymoon coordination and in-room dining, the idea is simply to rest after all those months of wedding planning. However if anything can entice you away from your love nest, it should be the stunning attractions of Spinalonga, Elounda, Knossos Palace, the pretty fishing villages, sailing trips or a dip in the crystal waters of the sea. Enjoy delicious, fresh food from the resort's à la carte restaurants and the mean cocktails in the glossy bay-side Crystal Box bar. You can even marry in a beach ceremony with a celebration meal on the chic terrace. Our favourite part? It has to be the Germaine de Capuccini wellness spa, with blissful thermal and hammam experiences. Do not miss the Cretan herbal and plant ritual using olive, argan and orange blossom oils for baby-soft skin. We can almost guarantee you will find yourself dozing off.

The Westin Paris-Vendôme

City of lovers, could there be anywhere more fitting to honeymoon than the unreservedly romantic Paris? With its neoclassical elegance piqued with a dash of modern glamour - all marble entrance hall floors, damson and dusky grey interiors, mirror and gilt-clad walls – The Westin Paris-Vendôme is a seminal hotel. Originally opened in 1878 and part of the celebrated Westin luxury hotel group, the hotel is grand and vast: but don't let this (or the fact that the beautiful salons frequently host Haute Couture fashion shows for the likes of YSL) fool you into thinking this is anything other than a restful and personal place. Brimming with plush comforts and cloaked in a hushed air of privacy, it answers all the requirements of a perfect lovers' nest. It's not without reason that Westin's beds are trademarked as 'Heavenly' with their downy linens and crisp white sheets. When combined with a visit to Six Senses Spa and dinner in the boudoir restaurant Le First, it may take some effort to venture out at all. Set right in the heart of the city overlooking the Tuileries Gardens and with chic fashion stores and art galleries nearby, it would be a crime however not to go out and share it all as newlyweds.

The Naka Island

While many honeymoon
hotspots focus on cultural day trips, The Naka
Island is all about doing absolutely nothing but
relaxing and soaking up the romance of being
newlyweds. Nestled in the Andaman South Seas
as it is peace, intimacy and a decidedly laid-back
attitude define this blissful resort. Just 25 minutes
from Phuket airport arriving by private speedboat,
the understated yet chic villas are surrounded by
fragrant coconut groves and feature white linen
canopied beds with bright colour accents. Slip into
a silken dress and sip cocktails on the shore, dine
on the freshest fish caught from the emerald waters,
laze in the spa for a couple's treatment – and if
you must venture out, take a trip to the South Seas
pearl farms of Naka Noi or visit James Bond island.
With eco-conscious credentials too such as 'green
housekeeping' to ensure Naka stays as special as it is
now, you could even host an intimate beach wedding
here on the sweeping white sands.

Château Saint Martin & Spa

As a delicately restored 12th-century fortress of the Knights Templar, a honeymoon getaway at the Château Saint Martin & Spa suggests a whole new level of sophistication and romance.

Tucked into the foothill shade of the Alps, yet just a short (convertible, please) car ride away from the coastal glamour of Cannes, Monaco and Cap d'Antibes or the Provençal medieval towns of Vence and Eze, the setting is almost too pretty. Secluded and sybaritic, we can think of no better place to unwind post-wedding and enjoy treats such as the La Prairie Spa and its new Bamford organic treatments, or getting a little merry with a private wine tasting in the cellars stocked with some of France's finest wines, or simply lounging by the pool following a scrumptious breakfast of artisan breads, almond croissants, cheeses and charcuterie. The high-end comforts don't stop at silk furnishings and Michelin-starred gastronomy either – don't leave without sampling head chef Yannick Franques' foie gras crème brûlée or sharing the local delicacy that is the blackcurrant tarte soufflée. The sleepy quiet of Château Saint Martin & Spa with its lavender-scented air and sun dappled setting marks this out as a heaven on earth hideaway for honeymooners.

Insider Tip

"While the fairytale villages and nearby towns boast Matisse adorned chapels, explore the surrounding countryside with a spot of horse riding, cycling or charter a yacht in true Cannes film star style – all of which can be easily organised by the Château's friendly team".

Secrets to Happy Ever After

The **Quintessentially Weddings** team share their personal snippets and tips on a long, happy and more-in-love-with-every-day-that-passes sort of marriage…

1. Treat each other with politeness, respect and humour. Do wear those naughty knickers every now and again.

2. We swear by dancing. Whenever we are feeling glum, or just because, we whack on some rock and roll and prance around the living room until we feel like we are those rock stars.

3. It is all about the edit: don't bog each other down with your daily gripes and whinges and always present a united front, whatever may be going on behind closed doors.

4. Whenever they are blue or irritable, Try a little tenderness, as Otis Reading had it.

5. Try to be a better man or woman for them. And never stop trying.

6. Trips to Paris. Now, in five years, spontaneously. Whenever.

7. As the old adage goes, where there is a willingness, there is a way.

8. A cook should never the bottle washer be! (If they cook up a mean dinner, you are on dish washing duty without needing to be asked).

9. Keep them on their toes by surprising them. A little love letter tucked into their briefcase, a shoulder rub with expert skills gleaned from a masseuse, doing the hoovering when they are out, secret baking sessions resulting in their favourite cake, cancelled meetings being replaced with spontaneous cocktail bar dalliances like days of old.

10. Sometimes secrets are good – as the author Siri Hudsvedt says, the thing you cannot get to is the thing that keeps you in love.

Anniversaries

Hell hath no fury like a bride or groom whose anniversary has been forgotten. With traditional benchmarks and gifts, keep them sweet with our guide to forgetting-them-not

1 Paper - think literature, love letters, artwork, airplane tickets and personalised stationery.

2 Cotton - bed linen, sweet nothings, a dress shirt and an invitation to dinner in a fancy restaurant.

3 Leather - bound journals, jewellery boxes, gloves and shoes.

4 Fruit and Flowers - a tree of the former for him, a painting or generous bunch of the latter for her.

5 Wood - heart-shaped chopping boards, a walnut photo frame with a lovely shot of you together in it.

6 Sugar - home-baked versions of their favourite cake, chocolates, candies and sweet liquors.

7 Wool - toasty knits, fine rugs from Luke Irwin, picnic blanket and a gourmet lunch packed to go.

8 Salt - decadent ones for the bath or salt scrubs, oysters, a sailing trip.

9 Copper - coloured leather handbags, pipes to a newly installed roll-top bath…

10 Tin - heart-shaped baking tins, biscuit tins, cigars in tin boxes.

15 Crystal - decanters, chandeliers, embellished dresses and whisky tumblers.

20 China - whimsical tea sets and sculptures, ceramic jewellery and cake stands.

25 Silver - Engraved hipflasks for a long country walk, silk pyjamas in mercury and elegant necklaces.

30 Pearl - strings of fresh-water pearls, an inlaid guitar, cuff links.

40 Ruby - anything the colour of which: jewels, trousers for him, and Port.

50 Gold - traditionally celebrated with a golden wreath, eternity rings, classic watches and gold-trimmed champagne saucers should do the trick.

55 Emerald - a trip to Ireland, membership of the National Trust, fine wine in a green glass bottle.

60 Diamond - you can never have enough

70 Platinum - matching signet rings, a jaunt in a silver Aston Martin, cocktail shaker…

THE
WEDDING
CONCEPTS

*Whether you dream of a big day defined by
a wildly glamorous setting and cocktails, or a
timeless reverie of muted colours in the city; from
the classic with a twist to the big day that fuses
high-fashion with exotic world touches, your
wedding celebrations start here with our ten
essential wedding concepts and secret address
books for each. Here is how to use them…*

Think About Your Favourite Things

Love haute couture fashion, walks in the countryside, live music, exotic island holidays or simply spending time in your own (beautifully decorated and covered in treasures) home? Use your daily life to inspire you when it comes to the key elements at the heart of your wedding. Write down your five favourite things from films to fashion designers, artists to flowers, and a picture should start to emerge.

Study Celebrity Nuptials

Did Kate Moss or Middleton's wedding make you swoon more and reach for the lace-edged hankie? Let the stars guide you.

Mix It Up

Do not be afraid to pick and mix elements from each to make your wedding utterly your own – if you love wild flowers and twinkling candlelight, but equally adore the high-octane glamour of a modernist venue blend the two or carry a thread from each by asking your florist to tailor your blooms to suit.

Work With Your Assets

Have a beautiful back garden available to you at your parents' country home, a natural flair for details or a collection of glittering vintage furnishings? Make the most of them by matchmaking your wedding style to what you have at hand.

Celebrate Your Individuality

All of the concepts are simply suggestions – discuss in depth with your fiancé what is most important to you about your big day and then find a middle ground that shines with personality, customised elements and fulfils all of your fantasies.

COUNTRY ROSE WEDDING

Packed with prettiness and with Elgar practically piped from the trees, the enduring appeal of the country wedding isn't hard to fathom. Deep in the lovely, leafy rural folds of the countryside lies Dewsall Court, an idyllic setting for a wedding weekend filled with artisan food, the sweet perfume of Philippa Craddock's roses and an undone elegance. If you're looking for a wedding that is as much about keeping things sweet and simple with hay-bales and chintz as it is about relaxed elegance, read on…

COUNTRY ROSE WEDDING

Dewsall

Few places match Dewsall for unapologetic rural charm and loveliness. Nestled in meadows of grazing sheep and wildflowers in Herefordshire countryside straight from Thomas Hardy, the scene couldn't be more idyllic. The estate's beautiful 17th century house itself is set in flower-laden gardens (we're talking soft English country blooms here of cornflowers, garden roses and foxgloves), surrounded by honeyed sandstone barns and a sweet Norman church, St Michael's and All Angels.

Each Dewsall wedding is unique – a point on which the delightful family here who custom-create each wedding pride themselves. They purposefully limit the number of weddings to ensure each couple is thoroughly cared for, and are dedicated to making it as personal as possible. There is nothing run of the mill here. Blending luxurious heritage interiors with wood panelling, coats of arms and airy beamed rooms with an informal homeliness, the house can be set up for services and receptions. There is also the option of the open-sided Wain House barn; a warm and welcoming venue with its tree-trunk pillars, candles and log-burning stove and perhaps some outlying hand-cleaved yurts. Everything here makes for a truly private, spirited and romantic celebration: the key thing with Dewsall is the mix.

Food is wholesome yet exquisite, ranging from rustic feasts to seasonal wedding breakfasts of lavish courses prepared by the highly experienced chefs. All can be served on mismatched antique china for that eclectic yet pretty aesthetic so essential to the country wedding. Then, of course, there are the local artisan ciders – a refreshing take on a reception drink if you want to go all-out country.

Dewsall allow you to take over the house in its entirety as your very own private country manor for at least two days, something it would be hard to resist, we imagine. Arriving in time for a welcome tea to settle and sink into the elysian surroundings, a rehearsal dinner can be arranged to ease you into your wedding and is included in the hire price. After a relaxing breakfast, the wedding day begins in earnest, and is sure to be a Dewsall-shaped dream. Weddings can be held in any season; imagine autumn nuptials accompanied by golden and fiery red fallen leaves and roaring log fires, or spring when the ground is flushed by the buttery daffodils. One thing's for sure - this is not your average country house venue, but the loveliest version imaginable.

Phillipa Lepley

Almost as timeless as the notion of the quintessential 'English Rose', Phillipa Lepley's wedding gowns breathe pure romance into a wedding with their pretty femininity. Celebrated as one of the last great bridal couturiers, Phillipa is revered for her fondness for perfection. We think a wedding dress from the Phillipa Lepley atelier is the most exquisite garment you could lay eyes on. With her way of making dresses that balance grace and finery to such beautiful effect, every bride who wears a Lepley gown will feel like the fairest in the land.

From her flagship store in Chelsea – all French antiquities and golden sunlight - her team of 'petites mains' craft couture and made-to-measure wedding gowns using only the most deliciously luxurious fabrics: Phillipa was born and raised in Nottingham after all, the home of delicate English lace. The making of your gown requires a meticulous attention to detail worthy of any Haute Couture designer; since the French rose-point lace and silk taffetas, duchesse satins the precise shade of double cream and embellishments are all hand-stitched in-house.

Famed for their flattering dresses that cinch on average two inches from the waist, up to six fittings may be required for a couture gown with its traditional process of toiles and adjustment. Even the minutia of your posture and poise are accounted for to ensure it fits like a dream. Completion time varies between six months to a year (though the team are able to whip dresses up in a matter of weeks, so do not despair) so, revel in having a heavenly gown made for you and visiting this delightful shop for as long as possible.

Whilst fully customisable and ever-changing, the collection is consistently demure and chic. "It isn't about being a slavish follower of fashion trends - after all, you want the wedding album to stand the test of time - it is about simple elegance and sophistication", says Phillipa. The collection notably includes classic A-line ballgowns in duchesse silk with the aristocratic flourish of a knotted sash at the back, voluminous skirts that call for sweeping through meadows on your way to the parish church, sweetheart gowns with lace cap sleeves as well as ethereal, beaded Regency-feel gowns tinged with chivalric nostalgia (picture Keira Knightley, Rosamund Pike and Tess of The D'Urbervilles). Each wedding gown is beguiling, lovely, nuanced and achingly pretty. Whether you opt for fabrics in pure ivory or with a delicate silver adornment, we think there is no-one more qualified for creating perfection than Phillipa Lepley.

Philippa Craddock

Nothing says 'English Country Wedding' more than arrangements of tumbling blooms and fluffy posies. For the prettiest take on romance Philippa Craddock certainly comes up roses.

A favourite with the likes of Alice Temperley and Jenny Packham (whose enchanting, light and chic leitmotif she shares), Philippa designs and arranges some of the loveliest wedding flowers. From her base in the heart of rural Sussex, her teams travel afield nationally and to the continent too, creating odes to the rural idyll that is such a uniquely English phenomenon. Natural, dreamy and abundant, Philippa channels everything we love about understated floristry whilst keeping things elegant rather than rustic.

Where once country wedding flowers meant bundles gathered from nearby pastures, Philippa has injected bouquets and decorative big-day arrangements with fresh, luxurious style. Whether in muted palettes of antique rose, white and blush lilac, with flashes of indigo cornflowers and bright pops of lemon yellow or even gold, there is nothing of the ordinary here. Keep things romantically 'country rose' in style by hiring silver rose bowls and urn-shaped vases that Philippa has sourced from Italy, France and antique fairs. Pair with varying bunches from posies of anemones, sweet peas, scented jasmine and delicate

stocks, to spectacularly big, loose blooms of hydrangea, Old Dutch roses, peonies and towers of delphiniums. Such blooms look particularly heavenly spilling down the staircase of a country manor house. Alternatively, why not let more formal containers such as cut-crystal vases, heady fireplace swags and silver candelabra centrepieces

bring a dash of cosmopolitan chic to your country wedding? You could fill them with soft, scented greenery and neutrals like eucalyptus, viburnum, love-in-a-mist, ivory ranunculus and white roses.

One of the secrets to Philippa's success has been her relaxed, sweet manner and that rare personal touch – she looks after every couple from consultation to the big-day overall styling herself. With an inspirational blog and better still, a flower school recently opened at Pheasants Hatch for the hands-on bride, that offers

scrumptious lunches and teas provided by a local Yotam Ottolenghi-trained chef.

Insider Tip

"For the country bride wearing lace, team your wedding dress with pure, crisp flowers in a small arrangement so as not to overwhelm. A hand-tied bouquet of white ranunculus looks super-pretty, as does a little cloud of gypsophila."

Lucy Davenport

When the woman behind some of the most luminously lovely wedding photographs utters the words: "Well, I have worked with Filippo Caroti and Mario Testino….", you know you're onto a winner.

Lucy Davenport proves that superlative style needn't be confined to the city. As a fashion photographer she brings her sense of composition and her eye for flattering angles, colour and poses to the picturesque beauty of the English countryside. Describing her approach as "observational", Lucy's images are fresh and full of the carefree, natural aesthetic we all yearn for on our wedding day. Preferring to melt into the background rather than direct couples too overtly, Lucy's all-seeing eye captures every detail, texture and moment. Light and sentiment are a signature with couples often embracing the notion of rustic romance, donning wellington boots and strolling through meadows to get the perfect shot as they perch on a kissing gate. All pictures are lovingly tweaked before being recorded to DVD and then of course, placed into gorgeous keepsake albums.

Offering engagement or 'love' shoots to get nervy couples used to the camera and to build their confidence (a given, thanks to her warm, friendly way), why not use your favourite photos from your shoot on Save the Date cards or scatter them throughout your guest book?

Biscuiteers

Baskets of flower-shaped biscuits, mini cakes and iced biscuits topped with butterflies and bumble bees: there's so much more to the country wedding cake with Biscuiteers. Take some of their charming riffs on the quintessential English biscuit, with biscuit-pops in sweet pastel shades. Every biscuit is hand baked with designs that can be personalised, too. There are also traditional sweets wrapped in cellophane for a nostalgic twist, from peppermint humbug ringlets, to raspberry soda fizzballs. We can't help adoring Biscuiteers' take on cheese and crackers most; with caraway or rosemary and parmesan button biscuits, paired with a heart-shaped cheddar and hot pear chutney, perfect for a country wedding supper snack.

Aspall

What could be more apt than sipping on a quintessentially British alternative to champagne for your reception drink, or even toast? Closer in nature to the fizzy stuff from the Champagne appellation than rustic English ciders, Aspall's long tradition of producing super-premium boutique cyders – think lighter, sparklier, more elegant – is borne out in this scrumptious, delicate appley drink that we like to call 'Champider'. Produced on the family estate in Suffolk following the rediscovery of an old family recipe in 2009, Cuvée Chevallier is double fermented for a highly refined drink with floral notes. Serve in coupes with a thin slice of apple or edible flower heads scattered on top.

CITY CHIC WEDDING

All cool and contemporary with fashion-forward key notes; this is the wedding in its most grown-up and glamorous guise. Don't stop at the Bruce Oldfield dress, but inject a neutral palette with bold pops of colour from your Manolos to your flowers. Switch up the wedding breakfast with a gastronomical feast from Marcus Wareing at The Berkeley following a cocktail hour reception - and set the stylish tone with invitations from Ruth Kaye Design.

Marcus Wareing at The Berkeley

For a memorable, fabulously indulgent take on a town wedding, why not embrace London's gastronomic scene with a wedding reception with Marcus Wareing at The Berkeley, and make food the focus?

After all, those parties and celebrations that linger longest in the memory are those that hit all of the multi-sensory soft spots; and Marcus's eponymous restaurant certainly ticks all of our boxes. When it comes to style, there are textures of velvet and lacquer with 'exploded' glass chandeliers, and of course, the wonderful aromas of double Michelin star cooking wafting around you, mingling with the happy chatter of your well-fed guests. Set in Knightsbridge's The Berkeley, a hotel as charming as it is coolly contemporary, we fell in love with the David Collins designed restaurant as soon as we clapped eyes on it. Only recently offered as a private, exclusive use wedding reception venue, the décor is pure Mad Men meets modern, understated chic. Think crimson walls, a white circle motif for that nod to swinging sixties graphic style, glass chandeliers and chairs in burgundy and black leather. You can put your own big day stamp on the space too with the help of the team, from place cards to menus, dining ware and flowers – the tables look prettily 'wedding' when dressed in piles of ivory Lily of the Valley and sprigs of blossom, or you can go all-out bacchanalian with tumbling grapes and punchy blooms. The main dining space holds 65, with an adjoining private dining room providing the perfect drinks reception space.

As you would expect, it is the food that really captivates and will make your wedding the one your friends and family talk about for years to come. Marcus began at the illustrious Savoy hotel, before training under Albert Roux and Gordon Ramsay, refining a rare talent for impeccable food. Passionately crafted for intensity of flavour before being presented in beautiful dishes to behold, this is joyous food. Bringing all that skill and feeling to creating your wedding breakfast, Marcus and his closely-knit team will devise a unique menu for your big day in collaboration with you. All of those wonderful meals you have had together can be used as inspiration to give the meal the most dream-like quality.

The house style of gastronomy blends inventive twists on great British ingredients with influences from around the world, but the common thread is super-fine dining. Seasonal menus feature Orkney scallops, Langoustine and asparagus, soft and sweet Cumbrian lamb with sweetbreads, quince and leek and the cheese board is to die for, laden with lovelies from La Fromagerie. The wine cellars house some of the best bottles in London from classic bin and vintages to lesser known treasures and fizz which can all be match-made to your menu: weddings simply do not come more delicious than this.

Bruce Oldfield

How to find a wedding dress

that combines a traditional sense of occasion with striking fashion freshness? The answer is easy.

"My one tip for a bride is do not throw away the chance to be the centre of attention. This is your moment; do not go into it half-heartedly", says Bruce Oldfield at his Beauchamp Place showroom.

Swathes of crisp white lace, acres of ornate hand embroidery and embellishment on top of a royal fan base: the appeal of a Bruce Oldfield wedding gown is enduring. The legendary couturier's creations encapsulate femininity with a sophisticated twist; timeless yet youthful and exceptionally beautiful – a wedding number from him is destined to become a modern classic.

Bruce Oldfield, OBE, has been creating dresses for some of the world's most iconic and stylish women for almost 40 years. Applying skills from a bygone age, his atelier produces dresses of supreme quality that make him the go-to designer for an impressive clientele. Many high-profile figures such as Queen Rania of Jordan, Samantha Cameron, Olivia Ferragamo and Jemima Khan have all been Bruce Oldfield brides. We have seen many dresses in our time, but few as fabulously exquisite as these. So, what to expect from a Bruce Oldfield wedding gown? A wide range of beautiful dresses in a variety of styles are housed in his bridal salon, with many statement creations to choose from. From fairy-tale ball gowns appliquéd with silk organza flowers, to glistening beadwork on bias-cut dresses, corded lace jackets atop voluminous tulle skirts; there is a spirited quality to these gowns and their perfectly fitted couture silhouettes. Each piece is distinctive in its own design, neither overly demure nor predictable. Add a statement veil and a floor-sweeping silk zibeline train and you will not fail to create an impact on your big day. The complete bridal line includes tiaras, shoes, veils, headpieces and jewels to finish the look.

Once you have decided on a Bruce Oldfield gown, there are a number of routes you can go down depending on your time and budget. Whether you opt for a custom-made gown from the current collection and have it made for you, a couture design with an array of fabrics, finishes and details to choose from, or an all-out special commission dress, you can be assured that the years of experience within the tight-knit team (and with Bruce himself of course) will guarantee the success of your finished dress. Special commission wedding gowns offer a couture experience, with Bruce and the bride jointly designing a variation on an existing style, or creating something totally unique. Traditionally, a wedding gown was a mark of

the bride's exquisite taste and of how wealthy, well-travelled, accomplished and fashionable she was. Whichever option you choose, these are real once-in-a-lifetime dresses.

Situated in the heart of Knightsbridge, Bruce's bridal salon is directly opposite his established couture showroom. The intimacy of the bridal space means that the entire process of choosing your dress is a comfortable, private and relaxed experience. As each gown is bespoke, everything is constructed to fit the bride and reflect her personality. This is managed through a series of fittings and, as everything bearing the Bruce Oldfield label is made in the atelier beneath his couture showroom, it is very likely that the seamstress fitting your gown is likely to be the one making it.

Hayford & Rhodes

Established in 1924, Hayford & Rhodes are London's oldest family florist with a rich history of designing flowers for some of London's most prestigious venues. The Rhodes sisters head up a team of highly talented florists who specialise in floral design for weddings. Every floral arrangement they touch exudes their trademark style that is as quintessentially British as it is unashamedly feminine. From luxurious table centres overflowing with clouds of hydrangea, blousy peonies and roses to delicate hand-tied bridal posies, the finished look is effortlessly chic. A case in point: a wedding at Merchant Taylors' Hall is classic Hayford & Rhodes with blooms in pretty pastel shades seemingly plucked from a Parisian patisserie. Small wonder that the team of sisters are our go-to for any uptown city wedding.

From the first, the process of designing your wedding flowers is a personal one, with the chance to collaborate on your plans in a private consultation with the friendly team. Perfected over months to ensure the arrangements balance style with romance, no two weddings will ever look the same thanks to an instinctive eye for setting and mood. Choose blooms to match your bridesmaids' dresses in colourful brights, or switch up the beauty with scented arrangements of sweetpea, freesia and rosemary.

Xander Casey

Just as effortlessly stylish as the city wedding is the gorgeous photography of Xander Casey. A society wedding photographer who ingeniously captures the moments you want to treasure, he is an easy-going, warm presence on the day. Discreetly snapping away in addition to taking more traditional group shots, Xander reflects that intangible mix of glamour, heritage and cool that is so typical of a London setting. Recommended by The Ritz, Claridges and The Berkeley's preferred photographer, no less, he creates fabulous images in crisp colour or black and white, making for the perfect album which you will oversee together over a glass of Champagne.

"My fundamental aim is to really capture the spirit and personality of everyone. To me, photography is all about being natural, spontaneous, and of course – having fun", says Xander. On the evidence of his relaxed, happy photographs, we would have to say he has nailed it.

Ruth Kaye Design

Think stationery has to be formal, staid and traditional? Think again. Primrose Hill based designer Ruth Kaye and her team of able accomplices are inspired by the vogues, nowness and glamour of fashion. And naturally by the city in which they beaver away in their chic showroom. Reminiscent of the couture houses of bygone eras, their bespoke stationery is as neat and refined as can be, but at the same time is always fresh, bright and modern. Kaye also possesses that rare knack for making everything feel thoroughly new and directional without ditching the appropriate etiquette of wedding stationery – none of the enduring appeal of a charmingly formal invite is lost. To look at them, one immediately thinks of Dior, of cool cocktail bars and a party you simply cannot refuse.

Working closely with you and your various suppliers from wedding planners to venues, dress designers, florists and caterers; the team ensure your style or theme is worked seamlessly into everything from the typesetting to the wording and textures. The watchword here is bespoke. There will never be another wedding nor invite like yours, and it is this versatility and originality for which we love them. Plus the quality of the goods themselves; heavyweight papers and high pigment inks, to tiny gilded lettering. Or, in the case of The Golden Ticket range, the paper itself is flecked with gold dust that shimmers under the surface. Little wonder then that Kaye's clientele range from rock stars to presidents (she won't name names, being a class act).

The line-up of stationery boasts colour-pop layered bright papers and card, beribboned pastels from the Romantic collection, LP records with their own sleeves, monograms or embossed motifs to bound volumes that tell your love story with all relevant inserts tucked into a leaf at the back. Invitations and their accoutrements of RSVP cards, maps and Wedding Registry cards are so

much more than just a first impression, after all. With gorgeous stationery, you can define your wedding's aesthetic and mood, whether it is an evocation of a vintage era or a bit of casual Left-Bank Paris understatement you are aiming for. As seasoned professionals with over thirty years collective experience, Ruth and her team are masters at balancing the quirkier elements that make your invitations feel utterly individual and unstuffy with the air of romance and occasion all good stationery needs.

All designs can be printed in any language - a must for cosmopolitan weddings in the city that can be printed on fully recycled materials. The best part is the pretty papers and cards are all from sustainable sources anyway (Livia Firth would surely approve), yet do not scrimp on that lovely feeling when you run your finger over finely milled paper, or the pop of the cerise on staggeringly pure white.

Armed with a stash of these crisp beauties, you cannot fail but to receive a flood of RSVPs with the 'yes' box firmly ticked.

Insider Tip
From Ruth Kaye

Invitations to social events were used by the aristocracy in England and France, beginning around the 18th century. High society would invite their peers to social events with hand written announcements composed by either the lady of the house, or the secretary, as writing was a mark of education.

Responses to these invitations would always be answered in your own handwriting on your own stationery; however as our lives became busier and busier, many of us no longer had the time to sit down and handwrite a reply. Since hosts and hostesses couldn't risk not knowing if their guests would be attending, they began sending reply cards with their invitations. Today they are sent with almost very wedding invitation that we print.

ROCK 'N' ROLL WEDDING

Be inspired by the iconic rock 'n' roll spirit with a wedding that blends glittering style and laid-back romance. Here we show you how to keep it polished with intimate nuptials at Blakes London followed by a chandelier-swinging party with a Bright Sparks soundtrack and decadent Choccywoccydoodah cake. All in your Vivienne Westwood dress, naturally and a pop of leopard print Charlotte Olympia shoes to totally encapsulate the look. It's only rock 'n' roll, but we like it.

ROCK 'N' ROLL WEDDING

Blakes
London

Super seductive velvets, lustrous walls in night shades of jet and gold, and lashings of wild decadence - Blakes London is the only destination for a wedding spangled with glam rock stardust. Bringing a laidback yet heady allure to swinging Chelsea since 1978, Blakes is the go-to destination for those who love rock 'n' roll romance with a unique and stylish twist.

Perfect for any bride who yearns for glittering elegance and cool on their big day, there is quite simply nowhere better to channel your inner rock-star than here.

Often dubbed the 'original luxury boutique hotel', former Bond girl Anouska Hempel dreamt up the glamorous interiors. Full of exotic treasures snapped up on her travels to India, Egypt, China, Indonesia, and Italy and beyond. The rooms capture the essence of the Vogue-worthy wedding, with three licensed suites available to take over for a wedding weekend of revelry. Our favourite has to be the Corfu suite with its hazy gossamer whitewashed palette and mother-of-pearl inlaid furniture, reminiscent of the Rolling Stones' south of France bolt-holes. It accommodates just eight guests and makes for a setting as private as can be.

With their raspberry, smoky grey and French Empire antique adornments found in souks and bazaars in Marrakech and Indonesia, suites 007 and 003 also make for elegant options for hosting wedding parties of 40 and 15 guests respectively. You could even take over the restaurant, a bar serving fabulous cocktails and nightcaps, as well as the 'Opium den' Chinese room. The lacquered tiles with motifs of birds of paradise, feathers and 'trompe l'oeil' rococo walls make for an authentic oriental feel. Accommodating 80 guests, this makes the perfect setting for more riotous wedding festivities with a real wow factor. Whichever you choose, the creative and attentive staff here will ensure every last detail is as indulgent and individual as you could imagine.

The wedding breakfasts are innovative and bursting with flavoured fusions inspired by Japan; delicacies include salt and pepper soft-shell crab, potato soufflé with caviar and vanilla ice, black cod with miso and ginger and the most exquisite feast of Sushi finished off with coconut ice cream with lime and palm sugar courtesy of the acclaimed Head Chef Neville Campbell. Don't miss the chance to raid the wine cellars before partying the night away in your suite and crashing out in your four-poster bed. If you're looking for the ultimate rock 'n' roll hideaway venue for your wedding day, this is undoubtedly it.

Vivienne Westwood

There is only one thing better than a beautiful bride, and that is one who is a little bit naughty.

Something of a national treasure, Vivienne Westwood has unquestionably put all notions of staid tradition firmly to bed with her irreverent bridal gown collection. These are not your average polite wedding dresses, but as you would expect from this great British couturier renowned for her plaid ball gowns and sending Naomi Campbell flying in her wedge platforms, Westwood's wedding dresses are romantic and a little rebellious in all the right places.

The designer of choice for any self-respecting rock star bride. Her bold gowns carry a sense of stately occasion with undeniable beauty in their fit, fabrics, and rich couture spirit. Whether created in lashings of Italian duchesse silk or frothy scarlet tulle, every dress speaks of the designer's trademark rebel touch. As Vivienne herself explains, "My dresses allow you to project your personality, and are quite theatrical in the sense that they are real dresses, well-designed, and they give you a chance to express yourself. They are also inviting - people respond to them".

Each gown is handmade at the Davies Street atelier by a team of highly skilled seamstresses. The dresses speak of the aristocratic dressmaking tradition; as women would only have one or two dresses made a year, these had to be exquisitely made and spectacularly lovely to set her apart. From the minute hand-stitching to the bountiful weight of the skirts, each gown is created in consultation with the bride and tweaked to reflect her tastes and style. This ensures that every creation is an entirely unique piece of heirloom couture. Be it floor-length organza or intricate lace, Westwood's signature silhouette is created with boning, corsetry and skirts that explode from tight bodices into a riot of the purest silk or whip over the hips for a vampish wiggle. Each is a once-in-a-lifetime frock.

When searching for a dress that bridges the gap between fashion and fantasy we don't think you can go far wrong with Westwood. After all, regardless of how free-spirited a bride may be, she will still want to appear exquisite above all on her wedding day. Whilst Westwood may be considered an iconoclast, she can cater to the established bridal fairytale (see her Carrie gown, as worn by the infamous character) without ever risking becoming dull. Her gowns certainly make a woman feel extraordinary: there is something about the clutch of the bodices and the poise these numbers lend the body.

The 20-strong line-up boasts silk georgette corset dresses shimmering with sequins, delicate

lace draped bustiers finishing in soft column
skirts or a blockbuster taffeta ballgowns. Dusky
rose and burnished gold also make appearances
inspired by far flung lands and exotic bohemia.
For the truly daring bride, a swathe of matte
crimson taffeta with matching cathedral veil is
most effective. The common thread is brave,
grand and decadent – the epitome of rock 'n' roll
style. Yet these gowns never stray far from the
dream of all brides. Every gown is available in
ivory, after all.

Charlotte Olympia

Forget little ivory, sheeny satin pumps or anodyne sandals: Runaway Bride, the eponymous shoe line from Charlotte Dellal is full of designs so stylish they steal the spotlight. A firm favourite of ours for her standout blend of striking footwear silhouettes, old school approach to glamour and just the right amount of playfulness; these are spectacular shoes you can wear long after the big day. Fusing a neutral palette of nude and cream nappa leathers, soft satins and flashes of leopard print ponyskin or even coquettish red suede hearts, every style will rock a look whether you're a bridal purist, hopeless romantic or wild at heart.

The shoes are all handcrafted in Italy and are as supremely comfortable as they are gorgeous. The collection features 'island' platform pumps with distinctive fan detailing at the heel, pin-up girl sandals topped with kittenish bows to lace booties as well as a leopard print court shoe as worn by Charlotte on her own wedding day. And for that something blue? Every pair comes with a pair of stockings topped with cerulean lace.

Emma Franklin

This Central St Martins trained
designer hand makes some of the most romantic
and astonishing jewellery we've ever clapped
eyes on. Using time-honoured techniques in her
Clerkenwell studio set in the heart of London's
jewellery quarter, Emma Franklin produces
engagement rings and wedding bands to
commission from solid gold and precious stones
from inky sapphires to glittering diamonds.
Balancing exquisite detail with unconventional
style and a dash of baroque mysticism, wedding
rings have never looked so cool. Plus, there are
statement pieces from cufflinks to necklaces
strung with wildlife motifs and shotguns –
perfect for adding that little rock star flourish to
your big day outfit.

Rebel Rebel

Sometimes more is more;
opulent painterly colours, loose yet sumptuous
styles and the wild naturalistic beauty of
flowers at the fore. Established in 2000, Rebel
Rebel have fast become a go-to for their
passionate way with vivid, fragrant blooms and
gorgeous wedding arrangements that use the
best of seasonal and British flowers wherever
possible. There is nothing run of the mill here,
with experimental centrepieces, buttonholes,
bouquets and a masterful approach to clashing
hues of rich crimson and hot pink.

Choccywoccydoodah

A **smattering of fancy coloured** roses, frolicking cherubs, Sailor Jerry tattoo-style hearts and the infamous Beatles riff 'All you need is Love' emblazoned across a helter-skelter tower of unadulterated glamour: Choccywoccydoodah are the cake artists to thank for transforming the traditional wedding cake into something altogether more fabulous.

Far from the white-royal-icing-three-tier wedding cake culture, each of this scarlet-walled bakery cum chocolatiers creations is lovingly hand-made in molten chocolate. Pretty cakes are all very well after all, but the rock n' roll wedding needs a suitably rocking, decadent cake. These marriages of scrumptious sponge and glittering style borrowed (we suspect) straight from the enclaves of the Glastonbury VIP area have become our go-to for the spectacular centrepiece of the hipster wedding. Sponges laced with Sicilian lemon, treacly ginger, exotic coconut and cappuccino or the infamous deep and deliciously naughty chocolate cake are built into sky-high masterpieces with bands of truffle cream. Everything is made using the finest Belgian Couveture and locally sourced ingredients for creamy loveliness; and there's not an ounce of glycerine, icing sugar or frosting to be seen. Featuring gold baroque filigree swirls, ivory white chocolate roses in 'Petite Rococco Tiers' and even chocolate flowers in fondant fancy shades, a wedding cake is in

founder Christine Taylor's words, 'quite, quite bonkers', but in a very good way.

Choose from the wedding cake collection or go all-out opulent with a bespoke commission, working in collaboration with the artists to concoct and stud your cake with individual motifs, monograms or song titles. Your cake will be delivered to your venue the day before the wedding via a dedicated cake courier service.

The Bright Sparks

I t wouldn't be a rock 'n' roll
wedding without a proper rock 'n' roll band;
something The Bright Sparks revel in. A handsome
four-piece of highly experienced, professional session
musicians, they don't just get the party started. They
get people dancing on the tables; kicking off their
shoes and swinging from the chandeliers.

The band came together in 2003 with the express
mission to revolutionise the clichéd party band with
a set list that spans The Killers, The Rolling Stones,
Guns N' Roses, Prince, Roxy Music and the Kings
of Leon. There is nothing safe or jaded about these
cool chaps who are happy to learn new songs for
special requests and who usually play a two hour
set of energetic and thrilling songs. They do a pretty
convincing cover of nearly every great rock 'n' roll
anthem; even tailoring their set lists to suit the feel
or era of your choice for one rocking party.

BOHEMIAN WEDDING

What could be more sumptuous and stylish than a wedding set at the fantastical Babington House? Eclectic, arty and beyond beautiful, there's nothing like a boho wedding. By day it can be all about the heady blooms of cornflowers, roses and peony. By night, dance barefoot under the stars in your swirling Jenny Packham gown fit for a faery queen.

BOHEMIAN WEDDING

Babington House

There's only one thing we like more than a country bolt-hole wedding venue, and that's one with a bohemian twist. Shaking up the 'manor house wedding' in the sleepy enclaves of its rolling Somerset hills setting, Babington House is Grade II-listed idyllic finery and corbels on the outside, and rustic luxury on the inside. Packed full of stylish touches (recently rendered even more refined thanks to a little revamp) the interiors – all reclaimed tiles, grand open fireplaces, artwork from the likes of Tracey Emin and taxidermist Polly Morgan and chic French grey linen – are wildly romantic. Just as lovely are the 18-acre grounds replete with an outdoor pool flanked by natural stone so it seems to seamlessly slip into the surroundings, and a walled garden providing the House kitchen and the Cowshed Relax spa with fresh herbal and botanical ingredients (perfect for organic-loving brides).

Available to non-members year-round, the entire house can be taken over for weddings. You can opt for the charming neo-classical private chapel with its domed apse and white-washed walls, gilding and oak pews good for 90 guests, or for a civil ceremony in the gorgeous mirror-lined Orangery that holds 130 guests. The ceremony can be followed by a drinks reception on the lawn with canapés. You can spread over the Library, Log Room, Pool Room and make merry in the glamorous turquoise, chrome-topped Bar before sitting down to a wedding breakfast in the Orangery – which can be linked to the Log Room for up to 130 seated guests. With views over the gardens and lake, a wedding breakfast of three seasonal, locally-sourced courses and lots of fine wine can be served with sweeping banquet tables laden with glassware, twinkling candles and loose country flowers for a real bohemian feel. You can fill up on the scrumptious food before partying into the small hours thanks to the 'no curfews' policy.

The package also includes 'Midnight Munchies' with items on the menu such as the legendary mini Babington burgers and the best mini macaroni cheese this side of Little Italy. Children can also take advantage of the Teeny House packed with games, activities or crèche services for the littlest ones. Staying true to its luxurious heart, there are 32 gorgeous bedrooms decorated in hand-painted wallpapers and vintage furnishings to accommodate guests, with charming comforts of complimentary Cowshed products and sinking beds, too. For true romance, reserve the suite with the galvanised free-standing bathtub that's big enough for two for

a post-wedding bathe. In fact, why not arrive a day before your wedding and treat yourself to some relaxation in the refreshed Cowshed Relax spa with its steam room, sauna and aromatherapy rooms with your friends before a rehearsal dinner? We'd use any excuse to cosy up here for as long as possible.

Insider Tip

"Supply guests with a wedding survival-kit of miniature Cowshed goodies, before treating them to room service breakfast the morning after."

Akira Isogawa

Oh, Akira! With floating gossamer silk chiffons and heavenly embellishment, these gowns are as romantic and free-spirited as they come. Japanese-born Akira Isogawa's luminous wedding designs are shot through with a carefree quality typical of his adopted home in Sydney, blended with ancient sensibilities inspired by his native homeland. Akira brings a fresh outlook with his work: his wedding dresses positively sparkle in their beauty and possess a lovely sense of movement – perfect for the fashion conscious, bohemian bride (who just might wear a crown of flowers in her hair).

Each gown pays homage to the legacy of Japanese textiles and the wedding kimono; be it in the drape and lean lines, or in the hand embroidery of a group of Japanese 'petites mains' who work the threads on bamboo screens in an art form handed down through the centuries. There is a contemporary edge too, thanks to the feather-light silk chiffons and papery silks selected for their diaphanous transparency. When layered, the effect is lantern-like as light filters through the fabrics. Yet it is the mysterious and magical textures of hand-dyed embroidery stitched in lustrous patterns of feathers, birds, clouds and botany – with subtly layered tones - that really makes our hearts race. When sunlight strikes the silk threads,

they glisten like rippling water. With a fluid, deceivingly simple silhouette that are as bold as they are ethereal, Akira's gowns look so natural in wildly pretty surroundings.

His collections include strapless gowns with knotted fronts in dreamy chiffon, a gown spangled with asymmetric beadwork that looks like a smattering of stars at first glance. There are also Spiral Shibori gowns embroidered with plant motifs, embellished gowns with cloud-like lacy embroidery and cap sleeves that are designed to appear as if butterflies had landed on the shoulders. There are even black wedding dresses for the truly unconventional bride, strikingly softened with their tulle overlay. The highlights? A shoestring silk slip with dropped

waist gathering for a nod to 1970s bohemian glamour and the voile caped dresses adorned with golden beads or origami swallows.

Every Akira gown is individually hand-crafted, from its hand-dyed fabrics to the Japanese methods of fabric manipulation such as Spiral Shibori, when knots of twisted fabric create intricate shapes and glorious drapery. For the creative-minded bride who is searching for that dress that looks and feels like heaven on earth, the search is over.

Zita Elze

When it comes to swoon-worthy
sophistication and spellbinding wedding floristry,
Kew based floral artist Zita Elze is the name on
everyone's lips. These are romantic flowers to fall
in love with. Whether it is a bouquet that reflects
the bride's personality in delicate blooms of lace-
like fronds and rose buds, or 'mise-en-scene'
room adornments, Zita's love of the ethereal
shines through in all her work.

Fond of smaller buds on the cusp of opening
out, Zita blends natural materials of branch,
gossamer foliage, fine botany and fabric in
a fresh and modern way. The magical allure
of this finely-wrought flower work lies in
the dreamscape concept of blending Haute
Couture techniques with nature to create living
embroidery that clings to bodices - tiny Astrantia,
Rosa Jenna, Nigella, Ornithogalum and Scabiosa
heads, or towering centrepieces, chair covers
and finger-thin ribbons studded with miniature
blossoms. This imaginative approach has already
gained much acclaim and earned Zita a Silver-
gilt medal at the 2009 RHS Chelsea Flower
Show for her "A Celebration of Life" embellished
floral creations. Beyond this, creating a balance
of stylish, detailed arrangements to suit colour
scheme and theme marks Zita out as a florist
possessed of an exquisite talent for interpretation.
Her displays of fondant pastels punctuated with
vermillion and antique pink or verdant greenery
make for a strikingly dreamy feel, and can be
tailored to any venue.

Zita's work is not just a delight for the eyes,
but has real wow-factor for all the senses. The
lovely thing about flowers is their ability to fill
the air with the hazily seductive scent of the
garden or a woodland dell – and you should
look no further for ambient displays that dazzle.
These arrangements of pale pink roses, wild
strawberries, Diplocylos, Senecio Rowleyanus
and hyacinths will beguile even the most cynical
of wedding guests. This, after all, is the point of a
wedding - to sweep family and friends away on
a cloud of love - and Zita's creation of a stunning
wedding wonderland setting does just that.

There are also Hen days with Champagne
lunches at the Zita Elze Design Academy where
you can learn how to make corsages, bouquets
and centrepieces for the home – or even
intensive week-long courses in Zita's inspirational
world of wedding flowers for the hands-on,
creative bride.

ilovegorgeous

For bohemian prettiness at its best, ilovegorgeous wins on every count. With gorgeous dresses and accessories from velvet capelets to satin slippers and crystal circlet headbands, for covetable wedding fashion for flower girls and bridesmaids look no further. Made from delicious fabrics with subtle embellishment; with their background in fashion, friends Lucy Enfield and Sophie Worthington created the label in 2006 in a bid to dress little girls in chic and whimsical style. Cue silk gowns with pin tuck pleat detail in shades of dusky pink and moonbeam grey and dresses that evoke Marie Antoinette in her Petit Trianon era with silk sashes and lace-trimmed sleeves.

Brown Paper

Delicately twinkling gold-foiled lettering, polka-dot 'confetti' and beautiful textile-print lined envelopes; whether it's a bespoke commission to design a suite of wedding stationery spanning Save the Dates, invitations and sweet personalised thank-you notelets, Brown Paper are our hot pick for the loveliest wedding stationery. Cousins, friends and fellow designers Sarah Silver and Juliette Collins established their stationery design company with its 'less is more' knack for whimsical yet always chic style so perfect for the bohemian wedding. All stationery is printed in the UK and arrives in brown paper boxes tied up with ribbon.

Pomp de Franc

Bountiful folds of bright cobalt buttercream shaped into botanical forms topping buttery cupcakes; Valrhona chocolate towers that make a little like the leaning tower of Pisa (but are all the more quirky and delightful for it) and sponges in flavours as diverse as vanilla, pumpkin, hazelnut and red velvet. Oh, and did we mention the rainbow layered sponges too? Maker of fantastical, colourful and fanciful cakes that are as delicious as they are edible art forms, Katie Franklin of Pomp de Franc is one of cake's real rising stars and a go-to for any fashionable, bohemian bride. With a pleasing (and very English) affection for the slightly eccentric, when the former fashion student isn't rustling up cakes for the likes of Lanvin, Vogue, Stella McCartney and Mulberry she loves to turn her hand to creating gorgeous wedding cakes that are an excuse to marry for alone.

VINTAGE
WEDDING

Surrounded by the elegance of a bygone age,
Vintage weddings are quite possibly the most
romantic for all of their lustre and iconic style.
Go love-worn and authentic or glitz-laden
Hollywood golden era, which we imagine
here with a spectacular setting at The Savoy;
cocktails in the American Bar all dressed in
your coolly glamorous gown from The Vintage
Wedding Dress Company.

VINTAGE WEDDING

The Savoy

Immerse yourself in the splendour of a bygone age at The Savoy for a wedding every bit as glittering and chic as its surroundings.

Following a multi-million restoration in 2010, the iconic riverbank hotel overlooking the city's starry lights has recaptured that wonderful combination of Art Deco and English Edwardian lustre with an extra touch of brilliance for good measure. This hotel is steeped in such history that you can just visualise the stars who have partied at The Savoy over the years; Marilyn Monroe's treacle-like voice floating from the American Bar, Coco Chanel's chain-trimmed jackets tickling the marble table tops, Katharine Hepburn's naughty laughter above the tinkling of the piano. We think of The Savoy as the encapsulation of romantic vintage spirit and what could be dreamier than that on your wedding day?

There are more gilt-framed mirrors than Versailles can shake a stick at, twinkling Murano glass chandeliers, beautiful furnishings in a palette of blue, lilac, white, smoke and dove grey dotted with the occasional hit of gold. It all calls for a wedding inspired by the pageantry of the golden age of glamour: think Rita Hayworth curls for the ladies, top hats and tails for the gents and Cecil Beaton-inspired photography to capture the whole experience.

Marry in one of the three large banqueting suites, or for smaller weddings, one of the six private rooms all of which share the same seductive style and are fully licensed for civil ceremonies. Then comes the wedding party to end all parties – like a brilliant scene from a novel by F. Scott Fitzgerald. Picture your reception in the Lancaster Ballroom with a lavish wedding breakfast with this backdrop: a vision of forget-me-not blue framed by white stucco and lattice plasterwork with a little flourish of gold. The wedding breakfasts are exceptional with a menu of Chateaubriand steak with pommes soufflées or the à la carte menu for more intimate weddings. The Savoy also ably caters for kosher celebrations. After dinner retreat to the American Bar for one of the Savoy's infamous cocktails (and if you ask nicely enough, perhaps even your own bespoke wedding day concoction), before an evening of revelry.

The 268 bedrooms including 72 suites are, of course, one of the biggest draws of The Savoy with its 'personal service naturally' butlers and grand style. More than mere nostalgia, they are luxurious (but never showy) with discreet high-tech modern comforts, Le Labo toiletry treats and steam showers.

Insider Tip

"Given how hard it is nowadays to bring together your loved ones, why not hole up for a wedding weekend here and encourage your guests to do likewise? It's a nod to the high society weddings of old, and a fine excuse to put on the glamour for a little longer."

The Vintage Wedding Dress Company

'**S**omething old, something new' goes the rhyme: and a beautiful wedding gown from The Vintage Wedding Dress Company fits the bill. Bringing us everything there is to love about vintage (and not just for the nostalgic among us), the team at this appointment-only atelier are indispensable for any bride looking to blend timeless style and cool modern glamour. With silhouettes cut from fluid silk, hand-beading and structured one-offs, there are plenty of options for adding personalised twists. If you've got your heart set on the alluring style of Lauren Bacall or if you covet Lana del Rey's mid-century Americana look, these exquisite numbers are sure to set your heart beating that little bit faster.

Everyone on the The Vintage Wedding Dress Company team has a fashion background and the dreamiest rails of authentic vintage gowns are carefully sourced by Creative Director Charlie Brear. A special mention must go to the team's collective eye for styling (a service that is usually the preserve of a celebrity clientele) and the meticulous alterations service which ensures that your dress fits like a glove. With a constantly changing selection of romantic lace and slinky silk bias-cut gowns straight from the Fin de Siècle, right through to 1970s dresses with a scattering of rhinestone, crystal and sequin, these are some of the finest examples of vintage bridal fashion we've ever seen.

To complement the original pieces and for brides who want the aura of vintage without the nostalgia, Charlie has designed the Decades Collection which takes inspiration from their treasure trove of meticulously sourced original vintage textiles and the runway in equal measure. The line-up features distinctive styles in French rose point lace, silk floor-sweepers and embellished gowns to neat prom-style dresses in pleated chiffon with cinched waists. What's more, you can choose from

additions to style up your dress and turn it into a
unique design; with lace sleeves, feather or fur
shrugs or detachable over-skirts for added drama.
The vintage silhouette is just the start.

Teamed with a billowing veil and some lustrous
vintage jewels from Chanel, Christian Dior or
Givenchy, you need look no further for iconic
bridal style.

Gillian Million

A **vintage wedding can only**
mean one thing: sparkle. Vintage jewels or a
fabulous tiara can really lift a wedding gown, which
is precisely why we love Gillian Million so much.

From her gorgeous shop in Teddington (just outside
of London), Gillian has been designing bespoke
tiaras, headpieces, jewellery, hair pins and more
for over 12 years, and we've yet to find anyone to
surpass their twinkling beauty. Clients can relax in
the fabulous sitting room and enjoy a consultation
over a cup of tea. From the refinement of Art Deco
with marcasite flower adorned hair slides and
elegant jewelled hair bands, to 'Breakfast At Tiffany's'
inspired collars of pearls stacked high - whatever
your chosen style, jewels from Gillian are quite
simply timeless.

Played out in beautiful clusters of crystal, real pearl,
rhinestone, semi precious stones, lace and filigree
detailing, each delicate and dramatic piece is created
in London and designed to order. Perhaps the loveliest
feature is the chance of include something old and
new into your pieces, such as unique vintage
gems and even treasured family pieces. Gillian is
equally as known for her exquisite veils, with styles
ranging from Belle-Époque Juliet caps, to glamorous
1950s birdcage and crystal-dotted fingertip veils.

Insider Tip

*"We will ensure you don't end up being overly adorned
but rather, beautifully accessorised. Jewellery and hair
accessories are a perfect way to create individuality
and catch the light as the day moves into the evening.
A statement necklace makes for a subtle way to inject
some lustre, and prevents you looking quite so bare if
you're wearing a strapless gown!"*

Pinstripes & Peonies

If like us, you like your flowers bountiful and blousily romantic, you'll adore London florist Ruari McCulloch and the work of his Pinstripes & Peonies team. Embracing seasonal, understated blooms, these arrangements add to the timeless feel of a Vintage wedding without the chintzy overtones.

From bouquets to buttonholes, right through to displays for weddings both decadent in scale (eat your heart out, Gatsby) and intimate, these carefully crafted flowers are beyond elegant. Known for their charm and cheerfulness, the team will set to work designing your florals with a signature eye for chic style that comes into its own with colour and theming. Expect frilly posies of peonies, mantles of creamy hydrangea and amaranths or centrepieces of sweetly scented English flowers; but most of all, an utterly personal approach.

PINSTRIPES
&
PEONIES

EVENT FLOWERS

Jon Nickoll

Want a little of that glittering screen magic for your big day? Look no further than the talents of the man often called 'a hundred people in one', the multi-instrumentalist Jon Nickoll, a man possessed of silver-fingers and a velveteen voice that delivers goose bumps every time. With an impressive catalogue that spans jazz standards, standout Hollywood soundtrack pieces (we'll put ourselves out on a limb by saying his 'The Way You Look Tonight' is better than the original), his own compositions and cocktail lounge modern classics, his natural talent has landed him the coveted spot as resident pianist at the Savoy's American Bar. A position he shines in next to his faithful Steinway and always in fine tux-suited style.

Peggy Porschen

Cakes have always been at the heart of a wedding; a timeless and luxurious confection traditionally made using rich exotic fruits and nuts to symbolise prosperity and fertility for the happy couple. Cake trends shift much like those of the catwalk, but the lovely bespoke wedding cakes from namesake Peggy Porschen and her talented team stand alone with their hints of old-school glamour - and the delicious sponges contained within of course. We defy cake-lovers of any epoch to resist these beautiful towers covered in elegant iced elaboration that range from dainty sugar paste hydrangea petals to blush piped whorls and scrolls for a pretty update…

DESTINATION WEDDING IBIZA

If you dream of a casual, beach wedding with plenty of summer party spirit and guaranteed sunshine, Ibiza has made it an art. Trimmed with bougainvillea, flanked by brilliant azure seas as far as the eye can see and the scent of lemon-groves filling the air, you can host an intimate wedding in Aura Ibiza before dancing the night away with your loved ones.

FLIGHT TIME *2 hours, 15 minutes.*
WHEN TO WED *May to September.*

DESTINATION WEDDING IBIZA

Aura Ibiza

Nothing beats paradise for a wedding, and if you're a fan of vibrant sun-drenched beauty, this gorgeous venue should be top of your list. Situated in the north of the island amid vineyards and citrus groves, Aura is like stepping into an approximation of Eden – but with added glamour. While we'd love to keep this lovely place secret, Aura has recently gone through a update only to emerge as one of the most romantic wedding venues we've seen. No longer just a hideaway for the A-list likes of Sienna Miller, Jade Jagger and Kylie; the glorious natural backdrops are well worth travelling for alone. This is the place for leisurely lantern-lit wedding feasts set in the lemon orchards.

Catering to intimate gatherings over cocktails and canapés through to anything up to 200 guests, a wedding at Aura can be as rustic or extravagant (true to Ibiza style) as you like. The refined, home-cooked food has elevated Aura to the highest echelons of world-class destination weddings. With freshly caught fish, locally sourced, seasonal and wherever possible, using ingredients plucked straight from Aura's own fragrant kitchen garden, the wedding meals here are a happy mix of Moroccan, Mediterranean and Moorish influences. Dishes are infused with rose, pomegranate, preserved lemon and peppy herbs and they serve some mean cocktails too.

The service at Aura reflects a belief that no request is too big or too small, the friendly team will balance all the elements for your dream wedding. From the lush garden terrazzo designed by James Holderness bedecked with jasmine, violet bougainvillea and palm trees for an open-air wedding breakfast, to chill-out zones, the cocktail terrace with its copper bar and an elegant fumoir, Aura's outdoor spaces all offer shade and are indisputably beautiful. It just seems made for sipping daiquiris under a star-studded sky with your loved ones. Picture your wedding dress gently ruffling in the breeze and maybe add some Mediterranean elegance with tulle voile drapes and strung bulbs for a pretty bohemian feel. Post-ceremony, you can even take over the entire place as your own island retreat.

The purpose-built villa, with its glorious palette of peach, flamingo, gold and soft sand inspired by the sunset, is the perfect space to host one of Aura's world-class DJ friends to accompany you into the small hours. Little enclosed spaces with banquettes are perfect for curling up in and catching up with your guests, but with Aura's air of cool, it's a master-class in low-key luxury that's simply sublime for a wedding.

Insider Tip

"Really spoil yourselves by booking in to stay at Cas Gasi, just 15 minutes drive from Aura. Aveda products in the bathroom, understated rustic yet chic décor, a tranquil pool and a favourite for its tranquillity — it's the perfect honeymoon spot."

Matthew Williamson

What could be more goddess-like than a long one-shouldered, feather-light castaway gown?

Gowns as light as they are paradisical, Matthew Williamson's eponymous bridal designs turn our thoughts to sandy shores, Cyclades blue seas and sirens. Perfect for the sun drenched climate, brides can rely upon these gowns to float and stay cool. The fluttering feathers and free-flowing, languid silk chiffons inspired by the ancient cultures of Greece and Rome are glamorous yet easygoing. Artisanal rigour is matched with a lightness of touch that defines the mainline collections, although these luminous visions in Delphic white tulle, ostrich feather and silk were made for the escapist romance of the island wedding.

Referencing treasure, bohemia and armed with an otherworldly quality, the gowns range from cocktail-length feather trimmed soufflés that lengthen the legs, to Grecian column dresses in the breathiest silk tulle. Bandaged empire-line crossover bodices in silk devoré touched with pearls flow down to diaphanous skirts and emphasise bridal purity in cloudy colours of shell-white and coral reefs. There are hints of shimmer in the soft lustre of silk and the embroidered sequin embellishment of a simple shift dress.

Impact is in the detail: gilded paillette-faceted bodices, hand-beaded encrustations and Swarovski crystalline straps as well as in the silhouettes which are ethereal yet modern. These are 'statement' dresses made with natural materials that move lightly and beautifully in the breeze, with hems that graze the ankles - ideal for beach ceremonies. "The common thread is femininity", explains Williamson, and it is easy to see that these sinuous, spirited dresses epitomise sensual, exotic beauty and are a dream to wear up a palm-tree fringed aisle.

Guilty Pleasures

It all began with Sean Rowley and one cult radio show, branching out into a club night, album series and party lovers' hearts – but now available to bring your wedding their particular breed of unashamedly fun, glorious pop music. Playing a set that covers the full pop spectrum from the 70s to the present of all those songs you're supposed to resist but furtively love, pop classics and forgotten greats: the Guilty Pleasures team can bring the full experience to your Ibiza wedding with DJs, dance troupes and speciality performers for the party to end all parties.

Minna

By way of her Dorset countryside home, Finnish designer Minna Hepburn's range of vintage-inspired, luxurious ethical and green fashion and fabric furnishings are cannily perfect and pretty additions to a wedding. From romantic, bohemian gowns for mini maids and grown-up bridesmaids alike in enchanting prints or feathered textures to dreamy tulle flower-adorned crowns, Juliet-cap veils cinched with floral appliqué and floppy hats for a little Bianca Jagger style, brides can inject that little iconic Ibizan spirit into their big day look too. Minna also recently started offering home textiles of elegant lace fabrics by the bolt, table cloths and curtains perfect for draping your venue.

Hidden Ibiza

Planning a pre-wedding get together or simply looking for a little let-your-hair-down relaxation? Nestled just 50 metres from the honeyed sands of Cala San Vincente on Ibiza's north coast is this magical clandestine garden bar and party space worthy of Alice and her Wonderland. Run by cocktail and hotspot legends Chris Edwardes and Amanda Blanch (for whom every space they touch seems to turn to gold), this woodland meets casually chic space boasts a literature doctor who'll exchange your books for the perfect holiday reading, crazy golf, classic parlour games, an outdoor spa for blissful massages and children's pagoda play area by day. By night, expect the best cocktails on the island from classics served in hollowed out pineapples to edgy blends, and live music from Spanish guitarists or shimmering DJ sets. There is delicious English tapas and afternoon tea too, and the space can be taken over exclusively as a real hidden gem of a wedding venue.

Natalie Beth Harris

Natalie does not do schmaltzy or twee, but flawless, luminous photography that captures every little detail of your wedding - she understands that every moment is precious. Having lived and studied photography in Barcelona (she speaks fluent Spanish), Natalie has shot in many a destination from Italy to London. However her light-filled, tender photographic style is never more at home than when among the relaxed romance and azure skies of Ibiza. Unobtrusive, she shoots in an artistic, photo journalistic style with a real talent for modern portraiture. The result? Evocative images, each individually hand edited with love so that your photos make you want to laugh and cry, and take you back in an instant to those special moments of your big day.

DOLCE VITA
WEDDING

The home of true romance and star-crossed lovers, whether set in the tumbling, vineyard-blanketed hills of Tuscany or the rustic faded grandeur of a Sicilian villa, Italy is where superlatively chic weddings come into their own. Hands down one of our favourite wedding destinations, read on for how to plan your 'dolce vita' wedding with expert James Lord, see how the wedding dress can be given a 'molto' pretty spin with Stephanie Allin and fall in love with two of the most sumptuous, sun-drenched venues in the world, Palazzo Avino and Hotel Caruso.

FLIGHT TIME *2 hours, 45 minutes*
WHEN TO WED *All year round;*
cooler from November to March

DOLCE VITA WEDDING

Mediterranean Weddings

with James Lord

Our man in Italy, James Lord certainly knows a thing or two when it comes to planning a beautiful wedding. As a unique partner to Quintessentially Weddings, London-based James brings years of experience planning weddings in Italy. With its glorious architecture, paired with simple yet dazzling gastronomy and endless azzure skies, it's easy to see why James' love of the country has led to his specialising in orchestration of bespoke weddings there.

We have to agree with James when he defines the allure as "a combination of perpetual sunshine, the al fresco celebrations, the culture, the wine, the way Italians are almost as religious about their food as they are about style…". The molto-glamorous aesthetic so synonymous with Italy, certainly comes into its own with weddings: whether it's a grand villa venue with Titian painted ceilings and shimmering Murano glass chandeliers, or the way a table is set just so with a feast under a canopy of stars, it's all done in a simple yet chic way.

Don't expect the rituals or fuss you would get with an English wedding: you can ditch the rules and adopt a typically Italian approach to time and schedules. As temperatures soar throughout the day, late afternoon weddings are a must: cue long lazy celebrations afterwards and oodles of time to indulge in the company of your loved ones (and spoil them, too) often followed by wind-down parties equally as jubilant. Handling the cultural and language barrier on one's own can prove tricky, however; bartering prices is likely to inflame even the most sanguine of those infamous Italian tempers. Fortuitously, James is a master of negotiation whose insider and local knowledge has no end.

Insider Tip

"Always plump for the local food option. You simply must try the traditional millefeuille wedding cake, with its layers of sweetened cream, nuts and honeyed pastry which puts even the most decadent tiered confection into the shade."

Italian Wedding Ceremonies

Getting legally married in Italy can be quite a trial, hence most couples opt for a wedding planner who can jump through the hoops for them. Below, we outline the various ceremonies available to non-Italian citizens and how to deal with any quirks.

Catholic Weddings

If you are both practising Catholics, you can marry in a Catholic church in Italy, but you will need to obtain a Nihil Obstat from your local diocese signed by the presiding bishop. The service is delivered in Italian and you will be expected to say your vows in Italian, too.

Civil Weddings

You will need to register your notice of marriage with your local council before applying to marry in Italy. The ceremony itself can only be held in buildings owned or managed by the local town hall, (but these are often beautiful and sometimes even castles) and as vows are read in Italian if you are not fluent, you will need an interpreter.

You must show the following to the town hall before your wedding: Non-impediment certificate issued by your local council upon notice of marriage, birth certificates and passports for both the bride and groom, copies of witnesses' passports (unless you are using witnesses provided by the Italian town hall), and legal copies of any deed poll name changes.

Blessings and Symbolic 'Weddings'

Of course, you can always opt to marry in the country you reside in or legally marry in a civil ceremony in Italy before hosting a blessing or personal ceremony.

General Details

Weddings are traditionally held in the afternoon post-siesta time. Some locations have Protestant churches and synagogues for which you will need to provide appropriate documentation and obtain permission from your local parish or synagogue. In the place of paper confetti or flower petals, Italians usually throw rice, nuts or grain over the bride and groom – just be careful to ask guests not to pelt you as it can sting!

Palazzo Avino

Prepare to be dazzled.

If you're a fan of romance of the E.M.Forster kind, this is the wedding venue for you. One of the most grand and unashamedly romantic hotels in all of Italy, perched 350 metres up the white rock cliffs overlooking the natural beauty of the Amalfi coast, Palazzo Avino (formerly known as Palazzo Sasso) has been one of the most desirable wedding spots since it opened in 1997 following restoration to its former glory.

Originally a 12th century home to the illustrious Avino and Ravello families, the blush stone villa with its Renaissance architectural features of high-arched windows and domed white porticos is nestled among the winding streets of the noble quarter of Ravello. Loved by literary types such as D.H.Lawrence, Virginia Woolf and the aforementioned Forster, Ravello became a playground for the stars of the silverscreen after Greta Garbo popularised this pretty medieval village, which retains all of its relaxed warmth and chic simplicity. There is just the right amount of Italian opulence at the five-starred Avino, with handpicked antiquities scattered throughout the 32 rooms and 11 suites against cool white marble floors and white-washed walls. Baroque gilt framed mirrors, original works of art, fine high-thread count bed linen, handmade Vietri tiles and modern luxuries of rooftop hot-tubs, Spa and a Lobster and Martini bar make for an aristocratic feel. Yet it is the backdrop to a wedding at Avino that renders us speechless. Just imagine your wedding ceremony on the marble-tiled rocky outcrop that seems to stand in the turquoise sea that reaches out to Salerno bay and the Sirens in the distance. Exchanging vows under a floating lace canopy to shade you from the sun, it doesn't get more secluded nor evocative than this. Lanterns can light the stairway back up to the palazzo as dusk falls, leading you up to an Italian-as-it-gets deliciously long wedding feast in either the dining suite or the terrazza overlooking the sea (we know which we'd go for, every time). Surrounded by the delicate fragrance of the bright fuschia and citrus blossom, Palm and Cyprus trees which look especially pretty strung with festoon lights for an authentic village plaza aesthetic; the star attraction of any Italian wedding has to be the food and the time taken to enjoy it, as at Avino.

Boasting two Michelin stars under executive chef Pino Lavarra, who trained with Raymond Blanc at Le Manoir aux Quat'Saisons, Avino's restaurant Rossellinis will cater to the most sumptuous celebration of your life with its beguiling flavours. Freshly caught seafood from the waters just metres away, homemade pasta and locally sourced ingredients combine in dishes that are at once simply Italian and

exquisite on the eye, too. Weddings at Avino can range from two to a maximum of 70 guests in order to ensure their spectacularly high standards. Such a dreamy venue and location are guaranteed to make you and your guests never want to leave, and Avino is certainly one of our best kept secrets. Why not take over the whole hotel for a three day long extravaganza, then honeymoon to make the most of stretching out on the beach or dipping into the plunge pools and drinking your way through all that (whisper it) staggeringly good wine filling Avino's cellars.

Stephanie Allin

Stephanie Allin's wedding
dresses are the perfect combination of sublime
femininity and classical beauty.

The designer is based in Wales and yet is heavily
inspired by cosmopolitan style and the silver
screen icons that have been the template for
effortless elegance since the fabulous fashion of the
50s. The sophisticated, lovely dresses are available
from her stores in both London and Wales. Inspired
by Audrey Hepburn and Grace Kelly with their
slit side pockets, lashings of lace and natty bow
waists. Stephanie is renowned for her way with
feminine curves and for creating a flawless fit and
feel that makes brides carry themselves with a
sense of majesty. Cleverly blending demure detail
such as sheer rose-point lace bateau necklines
over strapless duchesse satin dresses (as in the
gorgeous Kelly and Rosalba styles) with fittingly
sensational style, Stephanie's gowns are essential
for a wedding in Italy where opulence sits happily
alongside propriety.

The aptly named collections (notably La
Dolce Vita) work a treat for balmy al fresco
nuptials, and are light and carefree dresses to
wear in heat. From Ingrid, a narrow 'wiggle'
column gown with its silk-backed lace and
curved strapless bodice that sweeps over the
décolletage, to Gina, a proper va-va-voom
trumpet shaped number with halter neck

(reminiscent of Fellini's memorable Trevi fountain scene), the more sensual knockout numbers are still delicate and sophisticated. There are feather and subtle sparkling details on some with Gabriella's asymmetric crystal-studded straps giving the gown a Mediterranean goddess feel. Lace, the softest duchesse silk satins and taffetas really come into their own in the more vintage-feel dresses. Agi, a corded lace jacket cinched with a belt trim and Frankie with its crisp silk skirts and simple yet striking princess-line skirts are both perfect examples of chic bridal style. The stand-out gown has to be Mae, with its sinuous silhouette and detachable overskirt which you can keep on for wow-factor up the aisle, before whipping the skirt off for dramatic impact.

Hand made to measure in the atelier adjoining the original shop, there is a couture option and you can tweak nearly every style to suit, from adding little straps here to a few more centimetres to your train there. Simply add a billowing veil, some ornate earrings and a blush.

Hotel Caruso

Beyond the olive trees, bougainvillea and sweet-scented herbs of this idyllic Ravello demesne lies a classically beautiful restored 11th century former palace, and one of Italy's most uncompromisingly lovely and inviting wedding venues in our opinion.

It is partly the setting that makes Hotel Caruso so special – spectacularly perched on the tumbling green hillside of the Amalfi coast under a cloudless sky by day, and star-dusted by night. Maybe the chilled-out and warm atmosphere, frescoed ceilings and interiors that render class and sophistication, also have something to do with it. Mostly, it is the blissful celebrations of long, lazy reception banquets and the deliciously Italian spirit of a wedding here that pervades everything from millefeuille wedding cakes to the traditional honking of car horns to signal the start of your big day.

Available as an exclusive hire, the 50 rooms and suites with their sweeping views can be taken over in their entirety with accommodation for up to 200 guests within the hotel. The friendly staff are very happy to help you source additional rooms in neighbouring hotels should your party be a grand one. Lounge by the breath-taking infinity pool, take a boat excursion on one of the phalanx of yachts that bob on the turquoise water and dine on home-cooked, locally-sourced food that ranges from puff pastry cornets stuffed with truffled goats' cheese and pistachio shavings, freshly baked Neopolitan focaccia and limoncello ice-cream to cool. The appeal of hosting a wedding weekend with a rehearsal dinner on the terrace restaurant, a chic pool and cocktail party on the morning of the wedding before the ceremony followed by a candle-lit alfresco feast is obvious. When it is time for dancing, go barefoot around the pool…

Insider Tip

"Project cinematic classics inspired by your Italian setting onto a blank white wall for a little playful romance; think Fellini's Dolce Vita, or Roman Holiday".

HERITAGE WEDDING

Take inspiration from your favourite costume dramas and hire one of Britain's most glorious stately homes for a wedding full of oh-so-beautiful detail and more tapestries and corbels than you can shake a stick at. Woburn Abbey is just such a place, and teamed with an exquisite gown from one of the last great couturiers, Elizabeth Emanuel and painterly romantic flowers from Shane Connolly, here's how to give the royals a run for their money with a modern classic take on a wedding to go down in history.

HERITAGE WEDDING

Woburn Abbey Estate

To qualify as the definitive
heritage wedding venue, you need unbridled
period detail; you need to be surrounded by the
quintessential English beauty of the Humphry
Repton estate and a faint whiff of costume drama.
Luckily, Woburn has all of these in spades.

Classical beauty abounds throughout the 28
acres of garden where no fewer than nine species
of deer can be spotted roaming wild in the tranquil
grounds. The ancestral home of the Dukes of
Bedford is everything you could want from a
stately pile, and makes for a wonderful place to
celebrate. Inside the Abbey, the walls are awash
with masterpieces (from the likes of Van Dyck,
Reynolds, Canaletto and Gainsborough), exquisite
silks and chandeliers galore that all set the tone.
Queen Victoria was once a visitor, and really, who
wouldn't dream of an aristocratic-inspired wedding
here? It certainly possesses all of the romance of
a bygone age; for a wedding straight out of The
Duchess, this would be our venue of choice.

For the wedding itself, Woburn offers three
quite fantastic spaces including a Safari Lodge
in the heart of Woburn Safari Park populated by
lions, tigers and bears (oh my!). Yet the Sculpture
Gallery with its lake-side setting, private gardens
and sun-drenched marble is the star attraction.
You will find that the Gallery itself has an air of
privacy and tranquillity: you can host your civil

ceremony for up to 248 guests here before a celebration feast and dancing - 'heritage' doesn't have to mean sedate here that's for sure. Food is freshly prepared, with wedding breakfasts that deliver imaginative takes on great British classics and lots of Champagne. Get married in summer and you'll be surrounded by the beautiful estate in full, perfumed bloom or come winter, head to The Inn for a seasonal wedding. Woburn boasts a range of stunning backdrops including a neoclassical folly, the Chinese Dairy and the majestic 300-year-old cedar of Lebanon among its many wonderful settings for photographs.

Or, for a smaller, country-feel wedding, the 18th century Inn at Woburn is a delightful location for parties of 25 to 80 guests set on the edge of the

pretty estate village. Its gourmet dinner weddings for smaller parties continue to grow in popularity for brides looking for something small but special, and the hotel can also host civil ceremonies. Accommodation is pleasingly cosy and refined, with 48 bedrooms and 7 character cottages offered at the Inn – there are also the legendary 'morning after' breakfasts worth staying for alone.

Insider Tip
"As the home of the creator of 'Afternoon Tea' - Duchess Anna Maria, wife of the 7th Duke (who became tired with the hunger of waiting many hours between luncheon and fashionably late suppers and devised a light snack of sandwiches, cake and tea to tide guests over), why not tip your hat to this English staple by serving tea instead of a champagne reception, and offer Gin and Tonic cocktails as a fun twist on the T?"

Elizabeth Emanuel

Nothing quite surpasses the
romance and fantasy of grand gowns of
creamy folds in acres of silk, reams of lace and
stomachers (bodice fronts to you and I) adorned
with gilded beadwork that catch the light just
as they have done for centuries. With gowns
fit for and worn by a princess under her belt,
Elizabeth Emanuel's designs draw on the long
traditions and craftsmanship of haute couture;
marrying traditional fabrics, corsetry and
silhouettes that echo court dress straight out of
a Gainsborough painting.

Established in 1979 with her then husband
David Emanuel, the Anglo-American designer
took her Royal College of Art fashion training and
experience in theatre and film costumes, to create
arguably one of the most memorable wedding
dresses of all time for Princess Diana. However,
with the growth and nurture of her brand over
the following years, and the shift in fashion
away from the wild, flouncy romantic style that
prevailed in the 80s and 90s, the current crop of
astonishing gowns from the hands of Elizabeth
and her coterie of 'petite mains' are just as fitting
for the modern bride.

With all of the fitting sense of costume-drama
with rustling taffetas and oceans of silk trains, the
Elizabeth Emanuel bride is brought up to date with
a lightness of touch, a flash of décolletage there

(peeping through fine Chantilly lace, naturally) but no meringue-like fuss. Think boned bodices embellished with degradé organdie flowers and ribbons trimming the scooped neck of a strapless number before exploding into a skirt of soft tulle, ball gowns in blue-tinged silk plisse and cascades of flowers tumbling down bell-shaped skirts. Whether made to special commission or plucked from the current collection, these gowns make exquisite options for the thoroughly modern bride, who loves the drama, pomp and ceremony of a royal wedding - yet is, like a certain Duchess, in tune with the newer, more modest and nuanced mood of the times.

Insider Tip

"By tradition, a wedding gown was a mark of how wealthy and tasteful a bride was, and it was usually a jewel-coloured frock that she could wear again after the big day as an investment piece. This all changed in 1840, the year Queen Victoria is credited with starting the 'white wedding dress' trend with her pearly satin gown with lace adorning the shoulders and hem — but why not make like the brides of old with a softly coloured gown? They're surprisingly flattering, too."

Shane Connolly & Company

In Arcadian beauty and natural splendour, a wedding filled with Shane Connolly's sensitively crafted floristry stands second only to a royal one.

His company has long been the go-to for those in search of evocative yet disarmingly modest bouquets, centrepieces, buttonholes and boughs

that when orchestrated under talented hands, come together to create rich tapestries of wedding floristry. The company holds the royal warrant and indeed was behind the wedding flowers (those avenues of trees!) for TRH's the Duke and Duchess of Cambridge. Despite this, he and his team remain refreshingly discreet and utterly charming.

Heritage weddings hark back to bygone eras, and are sometimes too literal with their corseted gowns and fussy detail: Shane's talent bridges the gap between period drama and the simple romance of pure seasonal blooms. The result is always a unifying loveliness that sets the mood and interprets the vision he and his team work on intensively with each and every one of their clients. Every bouquet is designed to ensure a dress is not overshadowed, nor any venue out-dazzled by showy arrangements. The use of fresh bolted herbal heads from Catmint to Rosemary to blowsy garden roses symbolising love and virtue is inspired by a thorough knowledge of the chivalric Language of Flowers whilst also cunningly adding a perfumed, sensory link to the wedding's setting. Walking down the aisle beside pews trimmed with the crisp fragranced prettiness of apple blossom, Lily of the Valley and corn ears, it's hard to not be carried away.

Yet it is a rare knack for arranging flowers in a natural, organic way that is the star attraction with this firm's floral wedding masterpieces. Lending every display from the flower girls' head wreaths to statement garlands or blossom towers spilling out from urns as centrepieces for a dreamy aesthetic. There is something quite textile-like about these creations; like running your finger over damask, or pearl bead dusted lace. One of our favourite Shane Connolly leitmotifs is to trim venues with swags of foliage straight from the flower-trimmed tapestries

that adorn many a castle wall; there's just something so magical about it.

Devoted to humble wildflowers, their use of fragile but devastatingly pretty buds such as broom, wild carrots (Daucus Carota), primroses, snowdrops and bluebells makes for an easy fit between their distinctive taste for lovely green Englishness and immaculate artisan skills. When paired with a signature use of boxed trees, blossom festooned branches and bowls of pomegranate or oranges that mimic Elizabethan decadence (having travelled from lands afar); Shane Connolly & Company flowers provide the perfect foil to any venue. For that certain ravishing wedding floristry from days of yore mingled with airy fabulousness that is as vogue-worthy as ever, look no further.

Paul Antonio

In an age of email and e-vites, little beats the classic paper invitation. Especially when it is lovingly, lavishly scribed by master calligrapher Paul Antonio, whose clientele range from the style-setting (Kate Moss and Chanel) to the regal. Occupying an artisan's studio in London, this Trinidad-born gentleman has honed his craft via years of academia, research and what he calls 'playing around' with inks, genuine double density gold leaf and pigments to produce wedding stationery that is captivating, beautiful and unashamedly romantic. He's one of our most reluctantly disclosed secrets and here, Paul explains how caligraphy can be used for your wedding...

Why Calligraphy?

"With a long tradition that reaches back through the centuries, calligraphy has become a rare thing – handwritten correspondence just isn't something you see every day. I have always felt that if you understand and learn the purist way of doing things, this gives you the artistic freedom to be a little liberal, taking inspiration from eclectic sources – and this is where the bespoke nature of my invitations comes in. We can interweave a couple's story, their inspirations and even native language for the perfect hybrid of history, creativity and the personal."

The Process

"Initially, we ask couples to read through our 'Before you Call us' document that outlines the particulars of this lengthy, but oh-so-rewarding journey to ensure clients are prepared – calligraphy isn't for everyone, but if you love the proficient sweep of ink on velvety paper and want an invite unlike anything else you've ever seen, then you'll definitely hit it off.

You can opt to simply have envelopes addressed by hand in a manuscript-inspired script or go for the whole hog with Save the Dates, invitation suites, hand-drawn maps, monograms, cartouches, place names and table plans with menus written on paper or upon giant mirrors, orders of service, right through to Certificates of Marriage that evoke illuminated manuscripts. Either alone or as a set, your stationery should incite wonder every time it's looked at."

Firework Crazy

There is little else that is guaranteed to send guests of all ages in to rapturous rounds of 'ooh-ing' and 'aah-ing' quite like dazzling fireworks. A cracking team of firework professionals, Firework Crazy create wedding displays that blend technological precision and a fantastically theatrical sensibility with comprehensive service. From site visit to full public liability insurance, risk assessments and on-event care as part of the deal, you can commission an exuberant display of rockets, fountains, sky lanterns and even low-noise fireworks. The team can design your display to fit your colour scheme, include monograms or even sparkling hearts and an accompanying soundtrack from Marie-Antoinette inspired classics to medleys of rock n' roll or even film scores.

For that dose of fairy-tale magic that can only come courtesy of stardust-like fireworks shooting across the sky, look no further than these chaps who are as the name says on the tin - crazy about them.

WINTER
WEDDING

Once upon a time there was a bride clad
in white lace, pure as the driven snow, the
sparkle of antique chandeliers and the festive
warmth of a roaring log fire at Fetcham
Park – the winter wedding is pure fairy-tale.
Whether you want your wedding to enjoy
that fuzzy feeling of Christmas or the crisp
refinement of the season with hints of cut
crystal and jewel-like embellishment, winter
couldn't be more perfect for a beautifully
white wedding.

WINTER WEDDING

Fetcham Park

With its superlative beauty and ravishing period charm, Fetcham Park is one of those wedding venues we'd love to keep to ourselves, but equally, can't help telling everyone about. Having made its debut as a wedding venue in 2012, this Queen Anne house set in leafy Surrey is the stuff of big day dreams - and is run by surely one of the nicest family teams around as part of Parallel Venues.

The setting is romantic in that fabulously English way, and forms quite the first impression with extensive landscaped gardens, fountains and a portico. Built in 1705 with later additions of sweeping Georgian wings and a Chateau-inspired soaring slate-tiled roof, Fetcham is our favourite kind of wedding venue. It exudes a glittering style that harks back to an altogether glamorous era of champagne coupes, ball gowns and luxurious parties worthy of the most esteemed royal guests, all the while retaining a thoroughly free-spirited, fun atmosphere. The experience is a little like stepping into a country house party, as Fetcham Park is only ever hired on an exclusive-use basis.

The décor is just as elegant after a delicate update that has brought Fetcham back to life, with ice-cream shades of duck egg and vanilla lending fresh and pretty tones. The grand hallway leads to a dramatic oak staircase that makes for the perfect entrance for the bride, framed by painted ceilings and murals from Louis Laguerre (whose work also adorns the walls of Blenheim and Chatsworth, no less). The house itself offers three opulent licensed spaces for civil ceremonies. Take your pick from the Shell Room which can host 50 people for more intimate nuptials under a cherubic painted scene. Alternatively, there is The Salon complete with antique crystal chandeliers, stucco plasterwork dusted with gold-leaf gilding that showcase breathtaking style for a ceremony with up to 80 guests. Then of course there is The Great Hall, which can host 100 guests.

Whilst a wedding at Fetcham would be lovely whatever the season with flexible facilities for you to blend and use as you wish, we can't help but love it as an enchanting winter wonderland.

Just imagine a chic Christmas wedding here: the canopy of trees dressed in snow and the white blooms and thousands of twinkling candles. It is guaranteed to make you feel terrifically festive, particularly when celebrating your wedding with a scrumptious feast of seasonal food and warm spiced punch or mulled wine from the house's trusted caterers. Summer months may bring the chance to throw open those French doors to the lawns for a champagne reception, but few things can beat looking out over a snowy scene as you sit safely cocooned in the toasty, gentrified haven that is Fetcham.

Sassi
Holford

A **Sassi Holford gown**
is every winter bride's dream: equally as crisp
and captivating as the season of snow and pearly
skies, with skirts of soft silk and floating chiffon.
If you love the idea of feminine silhouettes
with the emphasis on delicate lace and bead
embellishment, you'll love Sassi's dresses.

Her Couture, Classic and Signature collections of wedding gowns effortlessly portray a very English elegance - no-one does classic romance quite like Sassi. Within her Somerset atelier, Sassi has brought together a team of professionals who expertly combine their skills on every garment with the same passion as their celebrated designer - and the bespoke, couture gowns are their masterpieces. Ballgowns with silk taffeta flowing over voluminous net petticoats, exquisite Chantilly lace beautifully framed by Sassi's gorgeous 'fit and flair' shape, and chic, fishtail gowns - they all personify Sassi's 'less is more' philosophy. It is this creativity in enhancing the female shape, whilst emphasising the bride's own personality, which allows Sassi bride to shine and feel at her most beautiful.

With over 30 years of experience, the self-taught designer-maker has a way with cut and drapery that exudes a sense of occasion. Though many British and European royal brides have passed through Sassi's Chelsea salon, she has remained as delightfully caring and unaffected as the day she discovered her natural talents in the art of the white dress. Sassi magically blends impact and style with exquisite detail. Whether you adore her little shrug jackets of lace fastened with pearl buttons or her

collection of sleeved dresses, (Sassi was there long before the Duchess of Cambridge) you can bask in wintry romance as Sassi did herself, marrying in the month of November.

From the made-to-measure collections in pure white to the couture gowns reminiscent of Grace Kelly's demure poise, these wedding dresses possess a vintage charm. There is an embarrassment of riches: plissé ball gowns cinched with crystal belts, duchesse satin gowns paired with corded lace bateau-neck shrugs, fluid silk gowns that are simply divine and, for the wow factor, sweeping skirts of silk poult beautifully finished with a deep, jewelled sash. Just picture one of Sassi's silk gowns with delicate guipure lace overlay, the hand-beaded cathedral train sweeping up the path to a venue straight out of Narnia, all silvery branches, twinkling candles and boughs of evergreens…

Quite the most graceful wedding dresses we've seen, Sassi Holford can outshine even the starriest of silent nights when it comes to pure beauty.

Insider Tip

"For that something old, a vintage marabou jacket is the perfect winter accessory for your gown - so cosy-chic!"

CJ Floral

Just when you thought a winter garden wedding couldn't get any more gorgeous, along comes the floristry of Chris Jones.

In keeping with his art and design background (and a botanist's understanding of flowers, judging by his regular Chelsea and Hampton Court Flower Show appearances) Chris creates enchanting arrangements with a painterly, almost textile-like quality. Ruffle-edged peonies meet hyacinth, roses, and lisanthus for a particularly painterly charm that is naturally decadent and extremely beautiful. Using seasonally appropriate blooms and an in-depth knowledge gleaned from experience helping his florist mother as a schoolboy, each bouquet and centrepiece is ingeniously constructed. From towering stems of blossom and emerald foliage to vases bursting with vital colour, Chris is widely loved for his adaptability, working on events both large (think royalty and the famous) to intimate and tiny. We can't think of a more green-fingered florist to perfect the fairy-tale bower look in winter weddings, albeit with a fabulously Erdem inspired feel.

Cellar Society

A **winter wedding calls for** toasty drinks full of spicy gusto yet grand elegance. Step forth Cellar Society's 'Mull-timate Mulled Wine' recipe given to us by creative director and founder Bertie de Rougemont as a complete exclusive, albeit minus one secret ingredient…

Inspired by the festive tradition of spiced wine started by the Victorians at yuletide, this mulled wine is like so much that fashion's favourite 'peripatetic restaurant' touches full of artisan, natural flavours whereby quality ingredients are allowed to shine. Think a menu of jersey royals topped with Oscietra caviar, saffron risotto with aged parmesan, Hoxton Sourdough sandwiches and damson sour cocktails for the likes of Louis Vuitton and Stella McCartney respectively.

Ingredients makes one serving

125ml Good quality hearty red wine (Cotes du Rhone or Malbec are good)
35ml LBV Port
10ml Brandy
1 to 2 teaspoons sugar to taste
5ml Lemon Juice
Mulling Spices to taste; we use the following per bottle of red wine
1 Cinnamon Stick
1 star Anise
1 scrape Nutmeg
1 Bay Leaf

2 Cardamom pods
2 Cloves
Garnish with an Orange wheel

Heat all of the ingredients in a pan till steaming, then leave to gently mull and infuse (without boiling) for half an hour.
Serve immediately, or let cool and bottle for reheating another day – it will keep for a week if refrigerated.

Cutture create such fantastical

winter wonderlands that they'll have you planning a winter wedding just to have an excuse to send some of their exquisite laser-cut invites. Turning heads with their striking pieces ever since their first wedding invitation commission in 2009, Cutture was conceived by husband and wife designers Helen and Dominic Sharland who share their Wandsworth Bridge design studio with a skilful team (who all share their boundless creativity and artisanal skills). Originally an exploration of how high-tech graphics could combine with whimsical illustration has translates into some of the most enchanting and inventive

Cutture's stationery and reception decoration pieces are intricate, delicate and above all, absolutely magical. Who wouldn't want a little of that for their wedding day?

wedding stationery we have ever seen. The bespoke design process takes your love story as its inspiration, from which the designers can work appropriate symbols, leitmotifs and city-scapes of places that hold significant meaning to you as a couple into your stationery. You could also opt to include lines from favourite songs or poems or your monogrammed initials, making for a truly personal invite. Yet nowhere is Cutture's own brand of magic more effective than when on the winter wedding stationery. Ethereal dioramas reminiscent of a Narnia snow scene, or festive stars and evergreens with your wedding venue as a backdrop are just some of the creative options. Normal paper turns into something quite extraordinary under Cutture's hands; etched

or filigreed acrylics become playful keepsake invitations. Choose from luxurious papers and cards, acrylics and mirrored Perspex which can all be layered to mimic classic fairy-tale images and add multi-dimensional appeal. The full range features pop-up boxed invitations, day and reception invitations with accompanying inserts, RSVP cards, table plans trimmed with laser-cut decoration, place-name cards trimmed with laser-cut detail, glass 'perchers', orders of service and calligraphy-inscribed menus on the chicest version of doilies ever dreamt up. Every item is printed digitally or using silk-screens, with hand-finished detailing to ensure crisp perfection.

SECRET GARDEN WEDDING

Love your style super-pretty and outdoorsy? Offering a fresh take on the classic garden party wedding and inspired by boutique festivals, Pearl Tent Company allows you to host a wedding in your nearest field or parents' backyard under one of their beautiful marquees adorned with armfuls of botanical blooms and a dreamy gown from Akira Isogawa. Always have brollies to hand, (white ones, please) in case the heavens open - and don't worry, it's traditionally a sign of good luck on a wedding day.

SECRET GARDEN WEDDING

Pearl Tent Company

Hidden away down flower-bordered paths, in a woodland dell or surrounded by a classically English lawn; a Pearl Tent is something to behold. As architecturally beautiful as they are robust, these spacious tents are constructed from crisp white canvas and can withstand even the blusters and vagaries of a British summertime. They have never once let us down and provide the perfect backdrop for the garden wedding.

Lashings of comfortable fixtures and furnishings mean that no matter where your secret ceremony or wedding reception may happen to be (there is no restriction on location) these structures wow. With the freedom to pitch among the surroundings of a country estate's rambling grounds, or perhaps the homely setting of your parents' garden; using one of Pearl Tent Company's structures lends a super-luxurious finish to even the most whimsical and wild of settings.

Available in 12 metre or 21 metre sizing; seating 120 or 200 respectively for a wedding breakfast; the tents themselves are generous and roomy. They are water and fire proof (thank goodness, as there's nothing lovelier than a lantern-festooned entrance). The tents are lined and can be hard-floored with carpet to provide a firm surface underfoot, with the choice of a traditional ballroom parquet dance floor or a kaleidoscopic illuminated version (yes please). With over 20 years of experience, the team behind The Pearl Tent Company will pitch and remove the tents with impeccable professionalism and can draft in furniture and lighting such as chandeliers or blazing torches to build your unique al-fresco venue.

After all, part of the joy of using such a blank canvas space for a wedding party in one of these tents are the options for dressing and creating a feel that is entirely your own. Be it a pretty bacchanalia with armfuls of loose, country flowers, greenery and rustic props, for a idyllic scene; the team can whip it together with linens, lace and even a Gin and Tonic bar. You can drape, adorn and light your tent up to your heart's content knowing that the setting will do all the hard work.

The Pearl Tent Company operates an April-to-October season: come dappled sunshine or the inevitable rain of a British summer, these tents provide a glamorous hideaway in which to lose yourself.

Insider Tip

"Take inspiration from what's around you and use flora in your food or to create hedgerow cocktails of Elderflower Champagne, Dandelion and Burdock Iced Tea or rose-infused Martinis."

Jenny Packham

Cast yourself as a sparkling, siren bride in Jenny Packham. Gowns as heart-stoppingly beautiful as they are bohemian, for dreamy romance meets Great Gatsby vintage decadence, these wedding dresses get us every time.

Inspired by the silver screen with their star-like embellishment and dresses dipped in Ostrich-feather trims they are fit for the languorous beauty of Ava Gardner and Vivienne Leigh. This being Jenny Packham after all, (loved by the likes of Florence Welch, Angelina Jolie and Kate Winslet no less), old-school red-carpet glamour always transcends.

Every dress shimmers with Art Deco style and sublime fabrics of bygone eras like floating, ethereal silk chiffon, the softest silk satins and fine French lace. Yet Jenny's trademark is in the astonishingly pretty detail. From silk gazar bias-cut goddess gowns gathered in soft pleats cinched at the waist with a pretty, crystal encrusted belt clasp, and a little lace peeking out from under the bodice, to a generous smattering of rhinestones and silver beads against oyster coloured chiffon - everything about these graceful gowns conjures magic. There is a modern freshness to the styles though, with a pale palette of blush, washed champagne and ivory played out in clean lines and fluid silhouettes made for sashaying down the aisle.

Our favourite has to be the exquisite Willow - all gilded beading, reminiscent of a woodland nymph with a touch of Kate Moss.

An alumnus of Central St Martins, Jenny's luxurious craftsmanship and hand-applied detailing has become legendary. You quite simply don't see such delicate or star-quality style any more, save for on a Jenny Packham number. From the chic bridal boutique which is like a little shot of Paris with its twinkling chandeliers, flowers and antique mirrors, your dress will be made to

metallic beads and gems so that you shine from every angle. That's the other thing with a dress from Jenny - no matter where the flash bulbs pop, there's something to dazzle. Designed with a knowing femininity the gowns are all incredibly flattering and easy to wear, as they skim over the body, hugging and flowing in all the right places. Whilst these dresses are so lovely they need little styling-up, one look at the glittering studded headpieces may well change your mind. There is also swoony, indulgent lingerie perfect for your trousseau…

Aruna
Seth

Here are some of the prettiest
bridal shoes (and we say that as women with more
than a mild footwear obsession) you'll ever see.
Designing shoes that fuse supreme comfort with
style, Aruna Seth hails from a family who work in
the shoe world. This may explain the incredible
attention to detail in her creations; but the talent
for producing stylish shoes is all her own. Taking
inspiration from the golden age of glamour
coupled with a playful and whimsical feel, how
about a pop of fuchsia, blush or even steel blue to
flash when you lift up your skirts to walk down an
outdoor aisle? "Match your shoes to your flowers
or go for an ethereal look with metallic or soft
ivory peeping from under your dress", says Aruna.
From hidden platform peep-toes to ballerina flats
or chic wedge heels, the perennial problem of
heels-sinking-into-grass needn't be one any longer.

The complete collection features Swarovski
crystal embellishment, twinkling seams running
up the heel of the shoes for a coquettish touch and
glittering butterflies perched on the toes. Made and
finished by hand in Italy using fine nappa leathers,
lace and satins, all the shoes incorporate plush
cushioning for ultimate wearability so you can
dance until the sun comes up.

Biscuiteers

Alongside their ranges of
delicious iced biscuit-pops, flowery mini cakes
and pretty woodland inspired biscuits; Biscuiteers
add enchantment to your wedding cake. Five tiers
of tempting sponge are adorned with emerald
foliage, butterflies, berries, daisies and flora and
fauna crafted from buttercreams and ganache for
a whimsical wedding cake. The stars of a secret
garden inspired sweets table are the personalised
favour biscuits, as well as the flower-power
cupcakes and butterflies that create a miniature,
edible cake bower.

Insider Tip

*"Keep any little ones happily occupied with a bake-
tent equipped with one of Biscuiteers' 'Cutter kits',
some balls of biscuit dough, aprons and rolling pins
for them to make their own treats. Ask your caterer
to whisk the biscuits off to the oven before icing; then
children can present them to their parents as a gift."*

Blistering

Nothing beats the inviting waft of fragrant wood smoke and the tenderest meat on a good barbecue. If you have visions of your wedding 'alfresco', surrounded by flowers and strung lights and a delicious selection of gourmet food cooked over wood-fired ovens or on an open-air grill, then Blistering are the caterers for you.

Their innovative menus range from traditional spit roasts of whole suckling pig or sweet lamb, (both sourced from Smithfield's finest butchers) to season-round feasts of bowl food or plated formal dining. Thus there is room for as elegant or as rustic a wedding breakfast as your heart desires. Blistering get the deep flavours spot on with innovative marinades, sauces and glazes. Cue sumptuous barbecues of spring lamb marinated in Persian spices, with parsley, mint and a ginger and rose petal jelly; chargrilled asparagus with buttery hollandaise, French-style herbed whole chicken and our favourite, butternut squash with warm spiced crust, goat's cheese, spring onions and toasted pumpkin seeds. Served with a swathe of salads to complement and bring out the flavours, Blistering can also theme your banquet for Indian, Oriental, Middle Eastern, Caribbean, tapas and Latin American styles. There are gorgeous puddings of tarts, giant Pavlovas and dense chocolate sponges while mixologists will whip up a luscious cocktail. We also love their oyster barrow for a touch of decadent fun...

iPower Cordless Lighting

Forget tea lights and candles blowing out constantly in the breeze; these are the bright and beautiful way to inject the outdoor wedding with a little refinement. A pioneering lighting concept using cordless eco-friendly bulbs, these stylish table lamps give you the freedom to scatter throughout your venue inside or out.

The collection, though constantly changing to ensure limited edition exclusivity (and moreover that no two weddings look the same), includes modern, period inspired and classic styles and shades in myriad colours that you can customise with your monograms. Our favourites have to be 'The Ritz' with a mirrored base and crystal drop pendant shade straight from a Great Gatsby and garden party, the romantic lines of the Portobella, a hand-crafted lamp with a twisted gilt base opening up into a magnificent tulip feature at the top. Whatever your choice of cordless lamp, there's no better way to add opulence to your wedding day.

Directory

ABSOLUTE FLOWERS AND HOME
14 Clifton Road, London, W9 1SS, UK
+44 (0)207 286 1155
shop@absoluteflowersandhome.com
Absoluteflowersandhome.com

ABSOLUTE TASTE
14 Edgel Street, London, SW18 1SR, UK
+44 (0)208 870 5151
info@absolutetaste.com
Absolutetaste.com

AKIRA ISOGAWA
Browns Bride, 12 Hinde Street, London, W1U 3BE, UK
+44 (0)207 514 0056
akira@akira.com.au
Akira.com.au

ALEXANDER MCQUEEN
9 Savile Row, London, W1S 3PF, UK
+44 (0)207 494 8840
Alexandermcqueen.com

ALLORA VISUALS
twitter.com/alloravisuals
+44 (0)795 857 0557
info@alloravisuals.com
Alloravisuals.com

AMELIA POWERS
+44 (0)785 001 2345
amelia@ameliapowers.com
Ameliapowers.com

ANETA MAK
Anetamakblog.com
+44 (0)778 897 2900
info@anetamak.com
Anetamak.com

ARUNA SETH
twitter.com/ArunaSeth
+44 (0)208 773 7859
info@arunaseth.com
Arunaseth.com

ASPALL
Aspall Hall, Debenham, Suffolk, IP14 6PD, UK
+44 (0)172 886 0510
Aspall.co.uk

AURA IBIZA
San Lorenç, Ibiza, Spain
+34 (0)971 32 53 56
info@auraibiza.com
Auraibiza.com

BABINGTON HOUSE
Babington near Frome, Somerset, BA11 3RW, UK
+44 (0)137 381 2266
reservations@babingtonhouse.co.uk
Babingtonhouse.co.uk

BISCUITEERS
18 Stannary Street, London, SE11 4AA, UK
+44 (0)870 458 8358
yum@biscuiteers.com
Biscuiteers.com

BLAKES LONDON
33 Roland Gardens, London, SW7 3PF, UK
+44 (0)207 370 6701
blakes@blakeshotels.com
Blakeshotels.com

BLISTERING
Streetfields Farm, Ford's Green, Nutley, East Sussex,
TN22 3LJ, UK
+44 (0)182 571 4712
info@blistering.co.uk
Blistering.co.uk

BOB WRIGHT MUA
+44 (0)783 406 6922
mail@botias.co.uk
Botias.co.uk

BOOTH NATION
7 Ezra Street, London, E2 7RH, UK
+44 (0)207 613 5576
info@boothnation.com
Boothnation.com

BOUCHERON
164 New Bond Street, London, W1S 2UH, UK
+44 (0)207 514 9170
contact.boucheron@fr.boucheron.com
Uk.boucheron.com

THE BRIGHT SPARKS
+44 (0)794 107 3289
info@brightsparksliveband.com
Brightsparksliveband.com

BROWNS BRIDE
12 Hinde Street, London, W1U 3BE, UK
+44 (0)207 514 0039
brownsbride@brownsfashion.com
Brownsfashion.com

BROWN PAPER
Studio 2, Spencer Court, 72 Marlborough Place, London,
NW8 0PP, UK
info@brownpaperdesigns.com
Brownpaperdesigns.com

BRUCE OLDFIELD
1st Floor, 34 Beauchamp Place, London, SW3 1NU, UK
+44 (0)207 584 1363
elizabeth@bruceoldfield.com
Bruceoldfield.com

BUCKLEIGH OF LONDON
83 Lower Sloane Street, London, SW1W 8DA, UK
+44 (0)207 730 0770
buckleighoflondon@hotmail.com
Buckleighoflondon.com

CAKES BY KRISHANTHI
Cakesbykrishanthi.co.uk/blog
+44 (0)208 241 2177
krish@cakesbykrishanthi.co.uk
Cakesbykrishanthi.co.uk

CASTLE ASHBY
Northampton, NN7 1LQ, UK
+44 (0)160 469 6696
sales@castleashby.co.uk
Castleashbyweddings.co.uk

HOTEL CARUSO
Piazza San Giovanni del Toro 2 84010 Ravello (Salerno), Italy
+39 089 858 801
info@hotelcaruso.net
Hotelcaruso.com

CELLAR SOCIETY
Unit 4, Falcon Park, Neasden Lane, London, NW10 1RZ, UK
+44 (0)208 453 7141
enquiries@cellarsociety.com
Cellarsociety.com

CHARLOTTE OLYMPIA
56 Maddox Street, London, W1S 1AY, UK
+44 (0)207 792 2884
customerservice@charlotteolympia.com
Charlotteolympia.com

CHATEAU SAINT-MARTIN & SPA
2490 Avenue des Templiers, BP 102 - 06142 Vence Cedex, France
+ 33 (0)4 93 58 02 02
direction@chateau-st-martin.com
Chateau-st-martin.com

CHOCCYWOCCYDOODAH
London, Carnaby and Brighton
+44 (0)127 332 9462
info@choccywoccydoodah.com
Choccywoccydoodah.com

CJ FLORAL
+44 (0)7966 164 278
chris@cjfloral.com
Cjfloral.com

COWORTH PARK
Blacknest Road, Ascot, Berkshire, SL5 7SE, UK
+44 (0)134 463 8530
information.cpa@dorchestercollection.com
Coworthpark.com

CUTTURE LONDON
269 Wandsworth Bridge Road, London, SW6 2TX, UK
+44 (0)207 751 8395
enquiries@cutture.com
Cutture.com

D&D LONDON
16 Kirby Street, London, EC1N 8TS, UK
+44 (0)207 716 7887
info@danddlondon.com
Danddlondon.com

DAIOS COVE
Vathi, 72100 Agios Nikolaos, Crete, Greece
+30 (0)284 10 62600
info@daioscove.com
Daioscovecrete.com

DANESFIELD HOUSE HOTEL AND SPA
Henley Road, Marlow-On-Thames, Buckinghamshire,
SL7 2EY, UK
+44 (0)162 889 1010
reservations@danesfieldhouse.co.uk
Danesfieldhouse.co.uk

DE BEERS JEWELLERY
50 Old Bond St, London, W1S 4QT, UK
+44 (0)207 758 9700
bondstreet@debeers.com
Debeers.co.uk

DEWSALL COURT
Callow, Hereford, HR2 8DA, UK
+44 (0)143 227 6724
info@dewsall.com
Dewsall.com

DJ PHILLY
+44 (0)795 611 0504
philly@djphilly.co.uk
Djphilly.co.uk

ELIZABETH EMANUEL
Art of Being Ltd, Garden Studio, 51 Maida Vale, London,
W9 1SD, UK
+44 (0)207 289 4545
info@elizabethemanuel.co.uk
Elizabethemanuel.co.uk

EMMA FRANKLIN
+44 (0)207 833 5855
emma@emmafranklin.com
Emmafranklin.net

EYELUSH
twitter.com/eyelush
+44 (0)752 553 6537
info@eyelush.com
Eyelush.com

FAUST'S POTIONS
3rd Floor, 207 Regent Street, London, W1B 3HH, UK
+44 (0)203 239 4633
info@faustspotions.com
Faustspotions.com

FETCHAM PARK
Lower Road, Fetcham, Leatherhead, Surrey, KT22 9HD, UK
+44 (0) 132 922 7447
info@parallelvenues.co.uk
Fetchampark.co.uk

FIREWORK CRAZY LIMITED
Unit 21 Eckersley Road, Chelmsford, Essex, CM1 1SL, UK
+44 (0)124 535 4422
mark@fireworkscrazy.co.uk
Fireworkscrazy.co.uk

FOX & ROSE
twitter.com/foxandrose
info@foxandrose.com
Foxandrose.com

GC COUTURE
411 Uxbridge Road, Hatch End, Middlesex, HA5 4JR, UK
+44 (0)208 428 8585
info@genuinecakes.co.uk
Gccouture.co.uk

GHOST
310 Kings Rd, London, SW3 5UH, UK
+44 (0)207 352 6460
Ghost.co.uk

GILLIAN MILLION
34 High Street, Teddington, TW11 8EW, UK
+44 (0)208 977 0588
info@gillianmillion.com
Gillianmillion.com

GREAT ESCAPE CLASSIC CAR HIRE
twitter.com/ClassicCarsHire
+44 (0)152 789 3733
info@greatescape.co.uk
Greatescapecars.co.uk

GREATHIRE
Unit 4 Bago House, 11-15 Chase Road, Park Royal, London,
NW10 6PT, UK
+44 (0)208 965 5005
info@greathire.co.uk
Greathire.co.uk

GUILTY PLEASURES
bookings@guiltypleasures.co.uk
Guiltypleasures.co.uk

HAWKSMOOR
twitter.com/HawksmoorLondon
+44 (0)207 481 6357
events@thehawksmoor.com
Thehawksmoor.com

HAYFORD & RHODES
5 Morocco Street, Bermondsey, London, SE1 3HB, UK
+44 (0)203 130 9219
info@hayfordandrhodes.co.uk
Hayfordandrhodes.co.uk

HIDDEN BAR IBIZA
twitter.com/HiddenIbiza
Hidden Bar Ibiza, S'Hort D'En Xic Busquets, Spain
+34 (0)971 32 02 53

HOUSE OF HACKNEY
41, Horton Road, Hackney, London, E8 1DP, UK
+44 (0)207 241 0928
house@houseofhackney.com
Houseofhackney.com

IDEAS BOX
Unit 11 Cranleigh Mews London, SW11 2QL, UK
hello@ideasboxuk.com
Ideasboxuk.com

ILOVEGORGEOUS
52 Ledbury Road, London, W11 2AJ, UK
+44 (0)207 229 5855
shop@ilovegorgeous.co.uk
Ilovegorgeous.co.uk

IPOWER CORDLESS LIGHTING
The Haven, Stoke Road, Lower Layham, Suffolk, IP7 5RB, UK
info@iPowerCordlessLighting.com
+44 (0)147 382 3218
+44 (0)752 519 8198
Ipowercordlesslighting.com

JENNY PACKHAM
75 Elizabeth Street, London, SW1W 9PJ, UK
+44 (0)207 730 2264
bride@jennypackham.com
Jennypackham.com

JO ADAMS MUA
twitter.com/make_up_jo
+44 (0)795 651 0382
jo_a_adams@hotmail.com
Getyourfaceon.co.uk

JO MALONE
150 Sloane Street, London, SW1X 9BX, UK
+ 44 (0)800 054 2939
Jomalone.co.uk

JON NICKOLL
+44 (0)207 794 1581
gary@garyparkes.com
Garyparkes.com

KAREN BEADLE MUA
twitter.com/#!/KarenBeadle
+ 44 (0)776 898 1421
karen@karenbeadle.com
Karenbeadle.com

KATIE FINE MUA
+44 (0)781 715 0763
katie@katiefinemakeup.com
Katiefinemakeup.com

KATY SCARLET TAYLOR
Twitter.com/straightupstyle
+44 (0)784 360 0979
katyusa111@hotmail.com
Straightupstyle.com

KATYA HERMAN
+44 (0)781 028 7620
katya@katyaherman.com
Katyaherman.com

LAURENT-PERRIER
Domaine Laurent-Perrier, 51150 Tours-sur-Marne, France
+33 (0)3 26 58 91 22
Laurent-perrier.fr

LEVIEV
31 Old Bond Street, London, W1S 4QH, UK
+44 (0)207 493 3333
info@leviev.com
Leviev.com

LILA
+44 (0)787 638 6391
contact@lila-lila.com
Lila-lila.com

LITTLE EGLANTINE
twitter.com/littleeglantine
+44 (0)203 287 0648
contact@littleeglantine.com
Littleeglantine.com

LITTLE VENICE CAKE COMPANY
15 Manchester Mews, Marylebone, London, W1U 2DX, UK
+44 (0)207 486 5252
info@lvcc.co.uk
Lvcc.co.uk

LUCY DAVENPORT
Facebook.com/Lucy.D.Photography
+44 (0)787 675 2495
info@lucydavenport.co.uk
Lucydavenport.co.uk

LUCY TANNER PHOTOGRAPHIC STUDIO
97- 99 Sclater Street, London, E1 6HR, UK
+44 (0)797 029 7988
lucy@lucytanner.com
Lucytanner.com

MACS SALON MAIDA VALE
61 Kilburn High Road, London NW6 5SB, UK
+44 (0)207 328 9777
macs.salon@gmail.com
Macs-salon.co.uk

MACS SALON PRIMROSE HILL
9 Princess Road, London, NW1 8JN, UK
+ 44 (0)203 204 2020
macs.salon@gmail.com
Macs-salon.co.uk

MAIDS TO MEASURE
+44 (0)207 386 9537
info@maidstomeasure.com
Maidstomeasure.com

MARCHESA
Browns Bride: 12 Hinde Street, London, W1U 3BE, UK
+44 (0)207 514 0039
brownsfashion@brownsfashion.com
Marchesa.co.uk

MARCUS WAREING AT THE BERKELEY
Wilton Place, Knightsbridge, London, SW1X 7RL, UK
+44 (0)207 235 1200
marcuswareing@the-berkeley.co.uk
Marcus-wareing.com

MATTHEW WILLIAMSON LTD.
46 Hertford Street, London, W1J 7DP, UK
+44 (0)207 491 6220
sales@matthewwilliamson.co.uk
Matthewwilliamson.com

MINNA
90 Brixton Road, London, SW9 6BE, UK
+44 (0)207 587 0887
minna@minna.co.uk
Minna.co.uk

MIRA ZWILLINGER
Browns Bride: 12 Hinde Street, London, W1U 3BE, UK
+44 (0)207 514 0039
studio@mirazwillinger.com
Mirazwillinger.com

THE NAKA ISLAND
32 Moo 5, Tambol Paklok, Naka Yai Island, Phuket 83110,
Thailand
+66 (0)76 371 400
naka.reservations@luxurycollection.com
Nakaislandphuket.com

NATALIE BETH HARRIS
+34 (0)652 69 36 93 (Ibiza / Barcelona)
+44 (0)774 779 2062 (London)
nataliebethharris@gmail.com
Nataliebethharris.com

No.4 HAMILTON PLACE
No.4 Hamilton Place, London, W1J 7BQ, UK
+44 (0)207 670 4314
aggi.bailey@4hp.org.uk
4hp.org.uk

NOBU BERKELEY ST
15 Berkeley Street, London, UK
+44 (0)207 290 9222
noburestaurants.com

NOBU LONDON
19 Old Park Lane, London, W1K 1LB, UK
+44 (0)207 447 4747
noburestaurants.com

NOTONTHEHIGHSTREET.COM
weddings@notonthehighstreet.com
+44 (0)845 259 1359
Notonthehighstreet.com

OLD FLAME
Etsy.com/shop/SiansOldFlame

PALAZZO AVINO
Via San Giovanni del Toro 28, 84010 Ravello, Amalfi Coast, Italy
+39 089 81 81 81
mariella.avino@palazzoavino.com
Palazzoavino.com

PAUL ANTONIO
Studio 6C, Clapham North Art Centre, 26-32 Voltaire Road,
London, SW4 6DH, UK
+44 (0)207 720 8883
paul@pascribe.com
Paulantonioscribe.com

THE PEARL TENT COMPANY
Upper Tilton Barn, Firle, Nr Lewis, East Sussex, BN8 6LL, UK
+44 (0)800 881 5377
info@thepearltentcompany.com
Thepearltentcompany.com

PEGGY PORSCHEN
116 Ebury Street, Belgravia, London, SW1W 9QQ, UK
+44 (0)207 730 1316
Peggyporschen.com

PHILIP TREACY
1 Havelock Terrace, London, SW8 4AS, UK
+44 (0)207 738 8080
studio@philiptreacy.co.uk
Philiptreacy.co.uk

PHILIPPA CRADDOCK FLOWERS
Pheasants Hatch, Piltdown, East Sussex, TN22 3XR, UK
+44 (0)182 572 3715
enquiries@philippacraddock.com
Philippacraddock.com

PHILLIPA LEPLEY
48 Fulham Road, Chelsea, London, SW3 6HH, UK
+44 (0)207 590 9771
info@phillipalepley.com
Phillipalepley.com

PINSTRIPES & PEONIES
+44 (0)773 980 8695
ruari@pinstripesandpeonies.com
Pinstripesandpeonies.com

PIPPA MACKENZIE
+44 (0)179 886 5483
pippa@pippamackenzie.com
Pippamackenzie.com

POMP DE FRANC
+44 (0)786 138 0945
Katie@pompdefranc.co.uk

PRESTIGE CARS
twitter.com/jdprestigecars
+44 (0)208 384 0795
info@jdprestigecars.com
Jdprestigecars.com

QUINTESSENTIALLY TRAVEL GROUP
29 Portland Place, London, W1B 1QB, UK
+44 (0)203 073 6673
info@QuintessentiallyTravel.com
Quintessentiallytravel.com

QMS COSMETICS
43 Cadogan Gardens, London, SW3 2TB, UK
+44 (0)207 730 8090
london@qmsmedicosmetics.com
Qmsmedicosmetics.com

ROYAL AIR FORCE CLUB
128 Piccadilly, London, W1J 7PY, UK
+44 (0)207 399 1005/4
confbanq@rafclub.org.uk
Rafclub.org.uk

THE REAL FLOWER PETAL CONFETTI COMPANY
Wyke Manor, Wick, Pershore, Worcestershire, WR10 3NZ, UK
+44 (0)138 655 5045
sally@confettidirect.co.uk
Confettidirect.co.uk

REBECCA STREET
Browns Bride: 12 Hinde Street, London, W1U 3BE, UK
+44 (0)208 995 5015
info@RebeccaStreet.com
Rebeccastreet.com

REBEL REBEL
5 Broadway Market, London, E8 4PH, UK
+44 (0)207 254 4487
mairead@rebelrebel.co.uk
Rebelrebel.co.uk

'RHUBARB' FOOD DESIGN LTD
5-25 Burr Road, London, SW18 4SQ, UK
+44 (0)208 812 3200
info@rhubarb.net
Rhubarb.net

ROSALIND MILLER CAKES
+44 (0)795 757 1797
info@rosalindmillercakes.com
Rosalindmillercakes.com

RUTH KAYE DESIGN
48 Chalcot Road, Primrose Hill, London, NW1 8LS, UK
+44 (0)207 227 7227
team@ruthkayedesign.com
Ruthkayedesign.com

SARAH CRITCHLOW
+44 (0)132 348 2624
+44 (0)780 143 2051
sarahacritchlow@gmail.com
Critchlowphotography.co.uk

SASSI HOLFORD
74 Fulham Road, Chelsea, London, SW3 6HH, UK
+44 (0)207 584 1532
Sassiholford.com

SHANE CONNOLLY
491 Latimer Road, London, W10 6RD, UK
+44 (0)208 964 4398
events@shaneconnolly.co.uk
Shaneconnolly.co.uk

SHARKY AND GEORGE
Studio 3 Crombie Mews, 11a Abercrombie Street, London,
SW11 2JB, UK
+44 (0)207 924 4381
team@sharkyandgeorge.com
Sharkyandgeorge.com

SMYTHSON
24/25 New Bond Street, London, W1S 2RR, UK
+44 (0)207 318 1610
Smythson.com

SNOW BUSINESS
The Snow Mill, Bridge Road, Ebley, Stroud, Gloucestershire,
GL5 4TR, UK
+44 (0)145 384 0077
snow@snowbusiness.com
Snowbusiness.com

STAPLEFORD PARK
Stapleford, Nr. Melton Mowbray, Leicestershire, LE14 2EF, UK
+44 (0)157 278 7017
weddings@stapleford.co.uk
Staplefordpark.com

STEPHANIE ALLIN COUTURE
81 Newton Road, Mumbles, SA3 4BN, UK
+44 (0)179 236 1477
stephanie@stephanieallin.net
Stephanieallin.net

THE DORCHESTER
Park Lane, London, W1K 1QA, UK
+44 (0)207 319 7071
groupandeventsales.tdl@dorchestercollection.com
Thedorchester.com

THE MANOR
Gerbestone Lane, West Buckland, Wellington, Somerset,
TA21 9PJ, UK
+44 (0)182 366 6297
knight@themanorsomerset.co.uk
Themanorsomerset.co.uk

THE RECIPE
Unit A, South Studio, Gainsborough Studios, 1 Poole Street,
London, N1 5EE, UK
+44 (0)845 130 8087
The-recipe.co.uk

THE SAVOY
Strand, London, WC2R 0EU, UK
+44 (0)207 836 4343
savoy@fairmont.com
Fairmont.com/savoy-london/

THE STATE OF GRACE
53 St Helen's Gardens, London, W10 6LN, UK
+44 (0)207 183 2729
info@thestateofgrace.com
Thestateofgrace.com

THE VINTAGE WEDDING DRESS COMPANY
33 Tottenham Street, London, W1T 4RR, UK
+44 (0)208 242 4380
enquiries@vwdc.co.uk
Thevintageweddingdresscompany.com

THE WEDDING SHOP
Selfridges: 400 Oxford Street, London, W1 1AB, UK
+44 (0)207 318 3094
Weddingshop.com

URBAN SOUL ORCHESTRA
+44 (0)208 968 3000
enquiries@urbansoulorchestra.co.uk
Urbansoulorchestra.co.uk

VALENTINO
Browns Bride: 12 Hinde Street, London, W1U 3BE, UK
+44 (0)207 514 0039
brownsbride@brownsfashion.com
Valentino.com

VERA WANG
Browns Bride: 12 Hinde Street, London, W1U 3BE, UK
+44 (0)207 514 0039
verawang@brownsfashion.com
Verawang.com

VIVIENNE WESTWOOD
6 Davies Street, London, W1K 3DN, UK
+44 (0)207 629 3757
Viviennewestwood.co.uk

WEDDING SMASHERS
+44 (0)207 249 7029
info@weddingsmashers.com
Weddingsmashers.com

THE WESTIN PARIS - VENDOME
3 rue de Castiglione, 75001 Paris, France
+33 (0)800 325 95959
reservation.01729@westin.com
Thewestinparis.com

WOBURN ABBEY
Woburn, Bedfordshire, MK17 9WA, UK
+44 (0)152 529 2172
sales@woburn.co.uk
Woburn.co.uk/weddings

WROTHAM PARK
Barnet, Hertfordshire, EN5 4SB, UK
+44 (0)20 8441 0755
info@wrothampark.com
Wrothampark.com

XANDER CASEY PHOTOGRAPHY
+44 (0)137 284 2522
xander@xandercasey.co.uk
Xandercasey.co.uk

ZITA ELZE
287 Sandycombe Road, Kew, Richmond, TW9 3LU, UK
+44 (0)20 8940 0040
zita@zitaelze.com
Zitaelze.com

29 PORTLAND PLACE
29 Portland Place, London, W1B 1QB, UK
+44 (0)845 475 8400
29portlandplace.com

Quintessentially Publishing Ltd.
29 Portland Place, London, W1B 1QB
Tel +44 (0)20 3073 6845
production@quintessentiallypublishing.com
www.quintessentiallypublishing.com

ISBN: 978-0-9569952-3-0

Acknowledgements

Author, Editor & Illustrator	Sophie Day
Editor in Chief	Caroline Hurley
Managing Editor	Hannah Matthews
Contributing Editor	Katy Taylor
Sub Editor	Nathalie Bradbury
Senior Designer	Giorgio Criscione
Designer	William Parry
Designer	Al Walker

With special thanks to: all of the team at Quintessentially Weddings, to our ever-supportive family and friends. The team in Quintessentially Creative, Patrick Fetherstonhaugh at Fetherstonhaugh Associates, Jessica Hailstone and Lee Wilson. Thank you to all our industry favourites who have allowed us to feature their companies and brands.

Photography Credits

Katya Herman	Jennifer Balcombe
Browns Bride, Aruna Seth, Pinstripes & Peonies, Wedding Diary, Anniversaries, 29 Portland Place	Aneta Mak
CJ Floral, 29 Portland Place, Katy Scarlet Taylor	Lucy Tanner
The Wedding Feast	Nick Matthews
About the Author	Alicia Pollett
Fubumedia	Rosalind Miller
Maids to Measure	Sam Pelly
Urban Soul Orchestra	Sim Canetty-Clarke
Culture	Calligraphy Paul Antonio Photography Eddie Judd
The Bridal Beauty Edit	Phillipa Lepley
Good Grooming, Big Day Survival Guide	Dewsall Court
Vivienne Westwood	Juergen Teller
Charlotte Olympia	Julia Kennedy